my **revisi⏻n** notes

Edexcel GCSE

COMPUTER SCIENCE

Steve Cushing

HODDER
EDUCATION
AN HACHETTE UK COMPANY

Hachette UK's policy is to use papers that are natural, renewable and recyclable products and made from wood grown in sustainable forests. The logging and manufacturing processes are expected to conform to the environmental regulations of the country of origin.

Orders

Bookpoint Ltd, 130 Milton Park, Abingdon, Oxfordshire OX14 4SB
tel: 01235 827827
fax: 01235 400401
e-mail: education@bookpoint.co.uk

Lines are open 9.00 a.m.–5.00 p.m., Monday to Saturday, with a 24-hour message answering service. You can also order through the Hodder Education website: www.hoddereducation.co.uk

© Steve Cushing 2017

First published in 2017 by
Hodder Education,
an Hachette UK company,
Carmelite House,
50 Victoria Embankment
London EC4Y 0DZ

Impression number   5 4 3 2 1

Year   2022   2021   2020   2019   2018   2017

Cover photo © Antonis Papantoniou/Hemera/Thinkstock/Getty Images

Typeset in Bembo Std Regular, 11/13 pts. by Aptara, Inc.

Printed in Spain

ISBN 978-1-471-886621

Get the most from this book

Everyone has to decide his or her own revision strategy, but it is essential to review your work, learn it and test your understanding. These Revision Notes will help you to do that in a planned way, topic by topic. Use this book as the cornerstone of your revision and don't hesitate to write in it — personalise your notes and check your progress by ticking off each section as you revise.

Tick to track your progress

Use the revision planner on page 4 to plan your revision, topic by topic. Tick each box when you have:

- revised and understood a topic
- tested yourself
- practised the exam questions and gone online to check your answers and complete the quick quizzes.

You can also keep track of your revision by ticking off each topic heading in the book. You may find it helpful to add your own notes as you work through each topic.

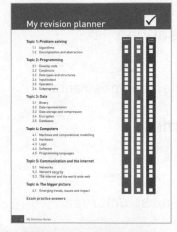

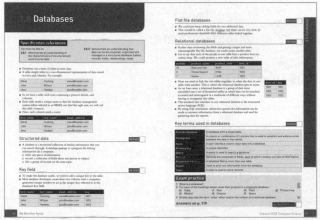

Features to help you succeed

Specification references

These lists tell you which points from the Edexcel specification are going to be covered in each section of this revision guide. You can also use them after you have finished each section to check that you know/understand everything you need to.

Exam tips

Expert tips are given throughout the book to help you polish your exam technique in order to maximise your chances in the exam.

Definitions and key words

Clear, concise definitions of essential key terms are provided where they first appear. Key words from the specification are highlighted in bold throughout the book.

Exam practice

Practice exam questions are provided for each topic. Use them to consolidate your revision and practise your exam skills.

My revision planner

Countdown to my exams

6–8 weeks to go

- Start by looking at the specification – make sure you know exactly what material you need to revise and the style of the examination. Use the revision planner on page 4 to familiarise yourself with the topics.
- Organise your notes, making sure you have covered everything on the specification. The revision planner will help you to group your notes into topics.
- Work out a realistic revision plan that will allow you time for relaxation. Set aside days and times for all the subjects that you need to study, and stick to your timetable.
- Set yourself sensible targets. Break your revision down into focused sessions of around 40 minutes, divided by breaks. These Revision Notes organise the basic facts into short, memorable sections to make revising easier.

REVISED ☐

2–6 weeks to go

- Read through the relevant sections of this book and refer to the exam tips and key terms. Tick off the topics as you feel confident about them. Highlight those topics you find difficult and look at them again in detail.
- Test your understanding of each topic by working through the 'Exam practice' questions in the book. Look up the answers at the back of the book.
- Make a note of any problem areas as you revise, and ask your teacher to go over these in class.
- Look at past papers. They are one of the best ways to revise and practise your exam skills. Write or prepare planned answers to the exam practice questions provided in this book.
- Try out different revision methods. For example, you can make notes using mind maps, spider diagrams or flash cards.
- Track your progress using the revision planner and give yourself a reward when you have achieved your target.

REVISED ☐

One week to go

- Try to fit in at least one more timed practice of an entire past paper and seek feedback from your teacher, comparing your work closely with the mark scheme.
- Check the revision planner to make sure you haven't missed out any topics. Brush up on any areas of difficulty by talking them over with a friend or getting help from your teacher.
- Attend any revision classes put on by your teacher. Remember, he or she is an expert at preparing people for examinations.

REVISED ☐

The day before the examination

- Flick through these Revision Notes for useful reminders, for example the exam tips and key terms.
- Check the time and place of your examination.
- Make sure you have everything you need – extra pens and pencils, tissues, a watch, bottled water, sweets.
- Allow some time to relax and have an early night to ensure you are fresh and alert for the examination.

REVISED ☐

My exams

Paper 1

Date:..

Time:..

Location:...

Paper 2

Date:..

Time:..

Location:...

1.1 Algorithms

Specification references

You must be able to:

1.1.1 demonstrate an understanding of what an algorithm is and what algorithms are used for and be able to interpret algorithms (flowcharts, pseudo-code, written descriptions, program code)

1.1.2 demonstrate an understanding of how to create an algorithm to solve a particular problem, making use of programming constructs (sequence, selection, iteration) and using appropriate conventions (flowchart, pseudo-code, written description, draft program code)

1.1.3 demonstrate an understanding of the purpose of a given algorithm and how an algorithm works

1.1.4 demonstrate an understanding of how to determine the correct output of an algorithm for a given set of data

1.1.5 demonstrate an understanding of how to identify and correct errors in algorithms

1.1.6 demonstrate an understanding of how to code an algorithm in a high-level language

1.1.7 demonstrate an understanding of how the choice of algorithm is influenced by the data structures and data values that need to be manipulated

1.1.8 demonstrate an understanding of how standard algorithms (bubble sort, merge sort, linear search, binary search) work

1.1.9 evaluate the fitness for purpose of algorithms in meeting specified requirements efficiently using logical reasoning and test data

Algorithms

REVISED

- An **algorithm** is a sequence of steps that can be followed to complete a task.
- A computer program is an implementation of an algorithm; an algorithm is not a computer program.
- **Computational thinking** involves learning how to use a set of problem-solving skills and techniques that are used by computer programmers to write algorithms.
- Computational thinking is about considering a problem in a logical way so that a computer could help us to solve it.

An **algorithm** is simply a set of steps that defines how a task is performed. It is a sequence of steps and decisions to solve a problem.

Computational thinking involves learning how to use a set of problem-solving skills and techniques that are used by computer programmers to write programs.

Exam tip

For the examination papers, focus on the sections covered in each exam paper as these will form the content of the questions on that particular paper.

Pseudo-code

Input and output are shown in pseudo-code as shown below.

Flowchart	Pseudo-code	Python 3
INPUT x	INPUT x	x = input( )
OUTPUT x	OUTPUT x	print(x)

> **Exam tip**
>
> A structure is a basic unit of programming logic; each structure is a sequence, selection or loop.

You can now create a step-by-step structured algorithm.

There are several advantages to designing solutions in a structured manner.
- One is that it reduces the complexity, as each set of steps can act as a separate module.
- Modularity allows the programmer to tackle problems in a logical fashion. Modules can also be reused.

More than one solution to any problem

- There will always be a number of methods to solve the same problem, but you always need to create ordered steps to use any of these solutions.
- We know there are many answers to the same problem, so what makes the best solution and would lead to the best algorithm?
- The first criteria we need to consider are:
  - Does the solution work?
  - Does the solution complete its task in a finite (reasonable) amount of time?
- We have lots of solutions to our problem and each, whilst very different, satisfies these two criteria.
- Therefore, the next step is to determine which of our solutions is 'best'.
- There are generally two criteria used to determine whether one computer algorithm is 'better' than another; these are:
  - the **space** requirements (i.e. how much memory is needed to complete the task)
  - the **time** requirements (i.e. how much time it will take to complete the task).

```
RECEIVE length, width, height FROM (INT) KEYBOARD
volume = length * width * height
SEND volume TO DISPLAY
```

> **Exam tip**
>
> Whilst you do not have to use the Edexcel pseudo-code in your answers, you must ensure that the pseudo-code you do use is easy for the examiner to understand.

> **Exam tip**
>
> An algorithm is a sequence of unambiguous instructions for solving a problem (for obtaining a required output for any legitimate input in a finite amount of time). A program is simply an algorithm that has been coded into something that can be run by a computer.

Trace tables

- A **trace table** is a technique used to test algorithms to see if any logic errors are occurring whilst the algorithm is being processed.
- Within the table, each column contains a variable and each row displays each numerical input into the algorithm and the resultant values of the variables.

We will look at this in more detail using a Python example:

```
y = 2                 #line 1; variable y = 2
x = 2                 #line 2; variable x = 2
y = y + x             #line 3
```

> A **trace table** is a method of using data to check that a flowchart or code covers all possibilities correctly.

Trace table:

Line	y	x
1	2	
2	2	2
3	4	2

Linear search

- A linear search is the most basic search algorithm you can have.
- A linear search **sequentially** moves through your collection (or data structure) looking for a matching value.

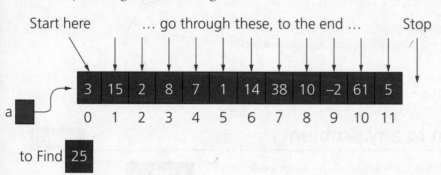

> **Exam tip**
>
> Do the easiest questions first. There is absolutely no reason to do the questions in the order they are printed in the exam. Getting one easy question complete at the start of an exam is a wonderful boost to confidence.

- In this case, we will not know that there isn't a record that matches the key until the end of the search.
- The number we are looking for is called the key. If we have a key of 3, we could show this as shown below, where each line is the next loop in the search:

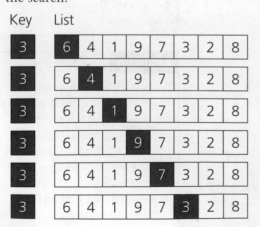

- When and if the code finds the key, it stops.

Binary search

- If we need a faster search, we need a completely different algorithm.
- The binary search gets its name because the algorithm continually divides the list into two parts.
- It looks at the centre value and disregards anything below or above what we are trying to find.

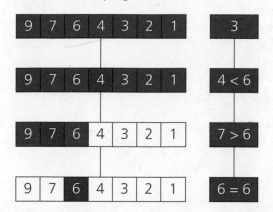

Exam tip

Don't forget to attempt all questions. The best way to gain high marks in an exam is to attempt all the questions.

- So each time you get to discard half of the remaining list.
- **But** the list has to be sorted before we can search it with binary search.
- To be really efficient, we also need a fast sort algorithm or to build the list in a way that maintains its order.

Comparing linear search and binary search

- Binary search requires the input data to be sorted but a linear search does not.
- Binary search requires an **ordering** comparison; linear search only requires equality comparisons.
- Binary search requires random access to the data; linear search only requires sequential access.

Exam tip

As long as the list is sorted, in almost all cases binary search is a more time-efficient algorithm than a linear search.

Sort algorithms

- There are a number of sort algorithms.
- As with searching, the faster the sorting algorithm, the more complex it tends to be.
- You need to understand two sorting algorithms:
  - bubble sort
  - merge sort.

Exam tip

Don't spend half an hour writing a long essay for two marks. It's a waste of time better spent on other parts of the question as you can still only get the two marks however much you write.

Bubble sort

- The simplest sorting algorithm is bubble sort.
- The bubble sort works by repeating (**iteration**).
- The **array** is sorted from the first **element** to the last by comparing each pair of elements in the array and switching their positions if necessary.
- This process is repeated as many times as necessary, until all of the array is correctly sorted.
- The worst-case scenario is that the array is in reverse order, with the first element in the sorted array starting as the last element.

> **Iteration** (looping) is repeating parts of a sequence over and over again, like eating breakfast every day at 7.30 a.m. It is the name given to the repetition of a sequence of computer instructions a specified number of times or until a condition is met.
>
> An **array** is a collection of data items that are given a single name and saved on a computer system in a sequential form.
>
> An **element** in computer science is an essential or characteristic part of something; other terms often used outside computer science are part, section, portion, piece or segment. An element can be an item of an array. Each element can be accessed by referencing its location in the array.

- Sorting takes an unordered collection and makes it an ordered one:

1	2	3	4	5	6
77	42	35	12	101	5

1	2	3	4	5	6
5	12	35	42	77	101

Merge sort

REVISED

- In merge sort algorithms the idea is to take an array or list and break the input into smaller pieces, sort the array or list on each of the small pieces, and then combine the pieces again.
- Once you have broken the problem into pieces, you break them down further into smaller pieces.
- The process ends when you are left with such small pieces remaining (for example, one or two items) that it is easy to sort them.
- Summarising, the main elements of a merge sort are:
  - **divide** the problem into halves
  - **conquer**: solve each piece by applying divide-and-conquer repeatedly (recursively) to them, and then
  - **combine** the pieces together into a global solution.
- Merge sort algorithms are a simple and very efficient algorithm for sorting a list:

> **Exam tip**
>
> If there are four marks available for a question, the marking scheme will probably have marks for four key points. Mention them all, and you get the marks.

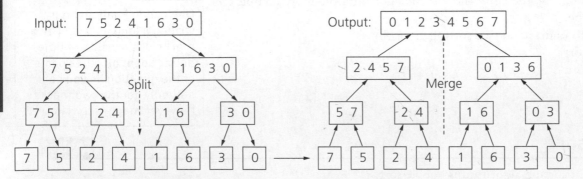

Comparing merge sort and bubble sort

REVISED

- In almost all cases, merge sort will take a lot less time than bubble sort to sort the data.
- Bubble sort is not efficient in terms of time but is quite good in terms of memory as the data is sorted within the list, whereas merge sort is much more time efficient but generally uses more memory as copies of the lists are created as they are split up.

Exam practice

1 The operation of processing each element in the list is known as? [1]
- **a)** Sorting
- **b)** Merging
- **c)** Inserting
- **d)** Traversal

2 Briefly describe a bubble sort. [4]
3 What is merge sort? [2]
4 The arranging of data in a logical sequence is called: [1]
- **a)** Sorting
- **b)** Classifying
- **c)** Reproducing
- **d)** Summarising

5 Write the pseudo-code where the user inputs the dimensions of a rectangle and the area of the rectangle is shown on the computer screen. [4]
6 Explain with simple examples the basic building blocks of coded solutions. [3]
7 Represent the following code as a simple flowchart. [4]

```
IF condition is true

THEN

    perform instructions in Action1

ELSE

    perform instructions in Action2

ENDIF
```

8 Design a simple flowchart to show the actions of a single move in a child's snakes and ladders game. [6]
9 In which language is source code usually written? [1]
- **a)** English
- **b)** Symbolic
- **c)** High level
- **d)** Temporary

10 State the main advantage of using a linear search. [2]
11 The worst case occurs in the linear search algorithm when? [1]
- **a)** The item is somewhere in the middle of the array
- **b)** The item is not in the array at all
- **c)** The item is the last element in the array
- **d)** The item is the last element in the array or is not there at all

12 The average case occurs in the linear search algorithm when? [1]
- **a)** The item is somewhere in the middle of the array
- **b)** The item is not in the array at all
- **c)** The item is the last element in the array
- **d)** The item is the last element in the array or is not there at all

13 Name two different searching methods. [2]
14 Briefly describe a linear search. [4]
15 Which of the following data structures does not use a linear data structure? [1]
- **a)** Arrays
- **b)** Linked lists
- **c)** Both of above
- **d)** None of above

16 Which of the following data structures uses a linear data structure? [1]
- **a)** Trees
- **b)** Graphs
- **c)** Arrays
- **d)** None of above

17 Finding the location of the element with a given value is known as? [1]
- **a)** Traversal
- **b)** Searching
- **c)** Sorting
- **d)** None of above

Answers on p. 114

ANSWERS CHECKED ☐

1.2 Decomposition and abstraction

Specification references

You must be able to:

1.2.1 analyse a problem, investigate requirements (inputs, outputs, processing, initialisation) and design solutions

1.2.2 decompose a problem into smaller sub-problems

1.2.3 demonstrate an understanding of how abstraction can be used effectively to model aspects of the real world

1.2.4 program abstractions of real-world examples

Decomposition and abstraction

REVISED

Two important techniques used in computational thinking are:

- **Decomposition**: This is breaking a problem into a number of sub-problems, so that each sub-problem accomplishes an identifiable task, which might itself be further subdivided.
- **Abstraction**: This is the process of taking away or removing characteristics irrelevant for the problem being solved in order to reduce it to something simpler to understand.

> **Decomposition** means breaking a problem into a number of sub-problems, so that each sub-problem accomplishes an identifiable task, which might itself be further subdivided.
>
> **Abstraction** is the process of removing unnecessary detail from a problem.

In computer science, abstraction is often used for managing the complexity of computer systems.

- The first step to solving any problem is to decompose the problem description.
- A good way to do this would be to **analyse** the problem.
- We can do this in simple steps.

Exam tip

You should always use a systematic approach to problem solving and algorithm creation, representing those algorithms using pseudo-code and flowcharts.

Exam tip

The key terms used in this guide are important as you will need to demonstrate your understanding of the correct terminology to gain good grades.

Input, output and process model

REVISED

A computer can be described using a simple model as shown. The **input** stage represents the flow of data into the process from outside the system. The **processing** stage includes all tasks required to effect a transformation of the inputs. The **output** stage is where the data and information flow out of the transformation process.

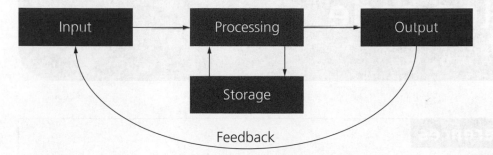

Feedback

Suppose we need to calculate the volume of a box given its length, width and height:

● First we identify all of the **nouns** in the problem.
● The nouns in the problem specification identify descriptions of information that you will need to either identify or keep track of. Once these nouns are identified, they can be used to identify:
  ○ input
  ○ output.
● In this problem we have length, width and height; these are our inputs.
● We have volume; this is the output.
● The word 'box' is irrelevant information for our algorithm. If we now identify all of the **verbs** in the sentence, in this case 'calculate', we have the process.
● So we now have:
  ○ inputs: length, height, width
  ○ process: calculate (in this case this is by multiplying the inputs)
  ○ output: volume.

> **Exam tip**
>
> Make sure that you fully understand the pseudo-code used in this book; it will be used in the coded examination questions.

Exam practice

1 Use pseudo-code to show how to receive data from a device. [4]
2 Use pseudo-code to show how to send output to the screen. [4]
3 What is an input? [2]
4 What is an output? [2]

Answers on p. 115

ANSWERS CHECKED

2.1 Develop code

Errors

REVISED

There are basically three types of error that computer programmers encounter when writing code. These are:

- syntax errors
- runtime errors
- logic errors.

Syntax errors

- A **syntax error** occurs when the programmer fails to obey one of the grammar rules of the programming language that they happen to be writing their application in.
- Whilst syntax errors usually prevent the program from running in some way, they are not easily found by a human.
- Typically, syntax errors are down to using the wrong case, placing punctuation in positions where it should not exist or failing to insert punctuation where it should be placed within the code.
- The most common syntax errors are as follows:
  - when the programmer forgets the quotes around a string
  - when the programmer forgets to put a colon at the end of an `if`, `elif`, `else`, `for`, `while`, `class` or `def` statement.
- You may also have a name error. This happens when you have:
  - misspelt a variable, function or method name
  - forgotten to import a module
  - forgotten to define a variable.
- You will need to be able to find errors in both your own code and the examination code, so you will need to understand how to do this.

> A **syntax error** is a mistake in the program's words or symbols, such as misspelled keywords, missing brackets or incorrect indents. These types of errors are the easiest to find. A syntax error is something that stops the interpreter from understanding the code (it cannot run).

Runtime errors

- A runtime error is an error that does not show itself until the program runs on the machine it is intended for.
- Good examples of this is when a program runs out of memory or when a website uses html code that is not compatible with the web browser being used, as these both often causes runtime errors.

Logic errors

- Out of the three common errors that occur in programming, **logic errors** are typically the most difficult kind of errors to detect and rectify.
- This is usually down to the fact that there is no obvious indication of the error within the software.
- The code will run successfully but it will not behave in the way it was designed to. In other words, it will simply produce incorrect results.
- The most common reasons for logic errors are as a result of the following:
  - the programmer did not understand the manner in which the program was meant to behave
  - the programmer did not understand the individual behaviour of each operation that was part of the program
  - careless programming.

> A **logic error** is something that stops the program doing what it is meant to do, or causes a runtime error (such as 'division by zero'). Logic errors are when a program works but does not give the answer you require, for example through using '<' instead of '>', adding when you should be subtracting, etc.

Testing

There are three types of test data:

1 **Under normal conditions.** The application is tested under normal working conditions with data within the anticipated range.

2 **Under extreme conditions.** The coded solution is provided with data that is within the operating range but at its limits of performance.

3 **Under erroneous conditions.** With tests under erroneous conditions, an application or program is provided with data that is outside its limits of performance. These particular tests try to break the application and to investigate if things occur when they shouldn't or vice versa.

Trace tables

- A **trace table** is a technique used to test algorithms to see if any logic errors are occurring whilst the algorithm is being processed.
- Within the table, each column contains a variable and each row displays each numerical input into the algorithm and the resultant values of the variables.

> A **trace table** is a method of using data to check that a flowchart or code covers all possibilities correctly.

We will look at this in more detail using a Python example:

```
y = 2              #line 1; variable y = 2
x = 2              #line 2; variable x = 2
y = y + x          #line 3
```

Trace table:

Line	y	x
1	2	
2	2	2
3	4	2

Efficiency

- There are many solutions to the same problem, so algorithm **efficiency** is important.
- Some algorithms are more efficient than others. It is obviously better to have an efficient algorithm.
- There are two main measures of the efficiency of an algorithm:
  - time
  - space.

Exam tip

Always stay on topic; if you're discussing the CPU, don't digress and start outlining other hardware.

- If it's possible to solve a problem by using what is called a **brute force technique**, you simply try out all the possible combinations of solutions.
- However, if you had to sort words with 158 characters when combined together including spaces, and you could compute 1,000,000,000 possibilities a second, you would still be left with the need for over 10^{149} seconds, which is longer than the expected life of the universe.
- So, to reduce time and make the algorithm more efficient, it is necessary to find a better approach.

Exam tip

Always review your answers. Proofread your answers as much as you can to correct any spelling mistakes and add any extra comments you think are worth mentioning.

Time measure

- Time measure is a function describing the amount of time an algorithm takes in terms of the amount of input to the algorithm.
- 'Time' can mean the number of memory accesses performed, the number of comparisons between integers, the number of times some inner loop is executed, or some other natural unit related to the amount of real time the algorithm will take.

Exam practice

1 What are the three types of error that computer programmers encounter when writing software? [3]
2 What is meant by a format error and what is its correct name? [4]
3 State what happens when programming statements are written in the wrong order, also stating the name for this type of error. [3]
4 Which type of programming error is the hardest to detect and why? [3]
5 What is the name given to the testing of software at the planning and flowchart stage? [2]
6 What is a trace table? [3]
7 What is correcting errors in a program called? [1]
   a) Compiling
   b) Debugging
   c) Grinding
   d) Interpreting
8 What is meant by the term 'algorithm time efficiency'? [1]
9 What are the two criteria that make for a 'good' algorithm? [2]
10 What are the two main measures for the efficiency of an algorithm? [1]
   a) Processor and memory
   b) Complexity and capacity
   c) Time and space
   d) Data and space
11 The time factor when determining the efficiency of an algorithm is measured by? [1]
   a) Counting microseconds
   b) Counting the number of key operations
   c) Counting the number of statements
   d) Counting the kilobytes of the algorithm

Answers on p. 115

ANSWERS CHECKED

2.2 Constructs

Specification references

You must be able to:

2.2.1 demonstrate an understanding of the structural components of a program (variable and type declarations, command sequences, selection, iteration, data structures, subprograms)

2.2.2 use sequencing, selection and iteration constructs in programs

The three combining principles (sequence, iteration/repetition and selection/choice) are basic to all imperative programming languages.

> **Exam tip**
>
> A theoretical understanding of condition(s) at either end of an iterative structure is required in the exam, regardless of whether they are supported by the language(s) being used.

> **Exam tip**
>
> Identifier names include names for variables, constants and subroutine names.

Variable declaration

REVISED ☐

- You can **assign** a variable a value on the same line as you **declare** it:
  ```
  int a
  a = 2
  ```
- This is the same as:
  ```
  int a = 2
  ```
- This is called **initialisation**.
- Variables only hold one value at a time:
  ```
  number = 1
  PRINT number
  number = 2
  PRINT number
  ```
- This will print:
  ```
  1
  2
  ```

> **Exam tip**
>
> If you run out of time and have two questions left to do, the way to maximise your marks is to do the first half of both of them.

- After these statements, the variable **number** will hold only the value 2 and not have any data kept about the value 1.

Constant declaration

REVISED ☐

- A constant declaration specifies the **name, data type** and **value** of the constant.
- Unlike a variable, a constant holds a value that **does not change**.

Assignment

- Assignment is the process of setting the value of a variable.
- A variable can be assigned different values during a program's execution – hence the name, 'variable'.

Syntax:

```
Variable R <add value here>
```

Examples:

```
Counter = 0
myString = 'Hello world'
```

Iteration

- **Iterations** are also called loops.
- Loops/iteration statements are used to repeat the execution of statements or blocks.
- There are two types of loop/iteration structures:
  - pre-test and post-test loops
  - loops that depend on reaching a maximum number of iterations or 'counts' (counter-controlled loops).

> **Iteration** is the name given to the repetition of a sequence of computer instructions a specified number of times or until a condition is met.

Pre-test loops

- The condition of the loop is tested **before** each iteration to check if loops should occur.
- Examples are **FOR** and **WHILE** loops.
- When encountering a pre-test loop, a computer tests the condition before the loop body executes.
- Programmers use pre-test loops when they are unsure if the loop might never need to execute at all.
- The loop has three parts:
  - The initialiser is executed at the start of the loop.
  - The loop condition is tested before iteration to decide whether to continue or terminate the loop.
  - The increment is executed after the test.

Example of a pre-test **WHILE** loop:

```
x = 0
WHILE x < 3
  x = x + 1
    SEND 'Hello' TO DISPLAY
END WHILE
```

Output:

```
Hello
Hello
Hello
```

Post-test loops

- A post-test condition is tested **after** each iteration to check if the loop should continue (at least a single iteration occurs).
- When encountering a post-test loop, a computer tests the condition **after** the loop body executes.
- Programmers use post-test loops when they want the loop body to execute at least once.

Example:

```
REPEAT
    OUTPUT 'Who will win the next World Cup?'
    INPUT userAnswer
UNTIL userAnswer = 'England'
OUTPUT 'You have wisdom.'
```

Count loops

- A **count-controlled loop** iterates a specific **number** of times.
- In Edexcel pseudo-code you use the following syntax for a count-controlled loop. The number of times **<command>** is executed is determined by the expression:

```
REPEAT <expression> TIMES
  <command>
END REPEAT
```

Example:

```
REPEAT 50 - Number TIMES
    SEND 'X' TO DISPLAY
END REPEAT
```

- In Edexcel pseudo-code you use the following syntax for a count-controlled loop using a step:

```
FOR <id> FROM <expression> TO <expression> STEP
<expression>
    DO <command>
END FOR
```

Example:

```
FOR Index FROM 1 TO 500 STEP 25
    DO SEND Index TO DISPLAY
END FOR
```

> A **count-controlled loop** iterates a specific number of times. In Python you use the **FOR** statement to write a count-controlled loop.

Selection

REVISED

- **Selection** is about making a decision. We have just shown a decision in the count loop.
- Decisions are usually **Boolean** so they can be true or false.

Let us say we want a condition where if a student's grade is greater than or equal to 60 we want the system to print 'Passed'.

```
IF grade >= 60 THEN
    SEND 'Passed' TO DISPLAY
END IF
```

> **Selection** is when a path through the program is selected based on a condition. Sequences are often not a simple line – often the next action depends upon the last decision; this is called selection.

We can expand on this code by adding an **ELSE** statement:

```
IF grade >= 60 THEN
    SEND 'Passed' TO DISPLAY
ELSE
    SEND 'Failed' TO DISPLAY
END IF
```

Nested loops

A **nested loop** is a loop within a loop.

> **Nested loops** consist of an outer loop and one or more inner loops. Each time the outer loop is repeated, the inner loops are re-entered and started again as if new.

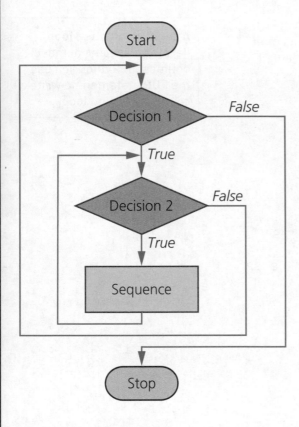

Example:

```
WHILE NotSolved
    <instructions here>
    FOR i FROM 1 TO 10 #this is the nested iteration
            <instructions here>
    END FOR
    <instructions here>
END WHILE
```

Modularity

- There are several advantages to designing solutions in a structured manner. One is that it reduces the complexity, as each set of steps can act as a separate module.
- Modularity allows the programmer to tackle problems in a logical fashion.
- Modules can also be reused.
- Modules are a type of subroutine. A subroutine is simply a sequence of instructions that is set up to perform a frequently required task.
- Code in a subroutine is **reusable**.
- A subroutine can provide a general solution for different situations.
- A well-defined task can be done in a subroutine, making the main script simpler and easier to read and understand.
- In pseudo-code you will need to understand the following:
  - IF
  - IF-ELSE
  - ELSE IF

IF

```
IF BoolExp THEN
    # statements here
END IF
```

Example:

```
a = 1
IF (a MOD 2) = 0 THEN
    SEND 'even' TO DISPLAY
END IF
```

IF-ELSE

```
IF BoolExp THEN
    # statements here
ELSE
    # statements here
END IF
```

Example:

```
a = 1
IF (a MOD 2) = 0 THEN
    SEND 'even' TO DISPLAY
ELSE
    SEND 'odd' TO DISPLAY
END IF
```

ELSE IF

```
IF BoolExp THEN
    # statements here
ELSE IF BoolExp THEN
    # statements here
# possibly more ELSE IFs
ELSE
    # statements here
END IF
```

Example:

```
a = 1
IF (a MOD 4) = 0 THEN
    SEND 'multiple of 4' TO DISPLAY
ELSE IF (a MOD 4) = 1 THEN
    SEND 'leaves a remainder of 1' TO DISPLAY
ELSE IF (a MOD 4) = 2 THEN
    SEND 'leaves a remainder of 2' TO DISPLAY
ELSE
    SEND 'leaves a remainder of 3' TO DISPLAY
END IF
```

Exam practice

1 Write the pseudo-code to output the numbers 1 to 50 inclusive using a WHILE loop. [4]

2 Write the pseudo-code to output the numbers 1 to 60 inclusive with a FOR loop. [2]

3 Briefly describe the term 'module'. [2]

4 Write the pseudo-code to ask the user to input values into two variables start and finish, then print the integers from start to finish inclusive using a FOR loop. [6]

5 Write the pseudo-code to ask the user to input values into two variables start and finish, then print the integers from start to finish inclusive using a FOR loop, but if start is bigger than finish output an error message instead! [8]

6 Write the pseudo-code to create a REPEAT-UNTIL loop for 1–6. [5]

7 Write the pseudo-code to create a WHILE iteration to output 1–3. [5]

8 Write the pseudo-code to create a FOR iteration to output 1–3. [5]

Answers on pp. 115–16

ANSWERS CHECKED

2.3 Data types and structures

Specification references

You must be able to:

2.3.1 demonstrate an understanding of the need for, and how to use, data types (integer, real, Boolean, char)

2.3.2 demonstrate an understanding of the need for, and how to use, data structures (records, one-dimensional arrays, two-dimensional arrays)

2.3.3 demonstrate an understanding of the need for, and how to manipulate, strings

2.3.4 demonstrate an understanding of the need for, and how to use, variables and constants

2.3.5 You must be able to demonstrate an understanding of the need for, and how to use, global and local variables when implementing subprograms

Data types and structures

REVISED

- Computers are machines that **process** data.
- Data is stored in the computer's memory in what are called **variables**.
- Variables have a **name**, **data type** and **value**.
- A variable is a **placeholder** of information that can usually be changed at runtime.
- Variables allow you to:
  - store information
  - retrieve the stored information
  - manipulate the stored information.

Exam tip

If you get stuck on a question, move on. Start doing another one.

A **process** is a series of actions or steps taken in order to achieve a particular end.

A **variable** is a name/location in memory/identifier, used to store a value which can change during execution of the code. The word 'variable' in programming describes a place to store information that can change, such as numbers, text, lists of numbers and text. Another way of looking at a variable is that it's like a box with a label on to store something.

A **placeholder** is a term referring to something not yet finalised. It is a section of computer storage reserved for information that will be provided later.

Primitive data types

REVISED

- The most common types of data, and the ones you will be using, are called **primitive** data types.
- Primitive data types are predefined types of data which are supported by the programming language.
- Data can be stored in many different forms; the proper term for these forms is 'data types'.
- In computing it is these forms that determine what actions, for instance searching, sorting or calculating, can be performed on the data when it is held within a field of a database or a spreadsheet.

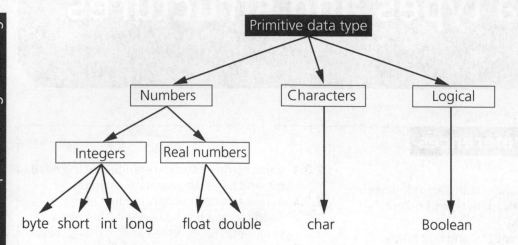

Integer types

- Integer data types deal with whole numbers, **not** decimal numbers.
- An integer can be **signed** (positive or negative) or **unsigned**; either type can be zero.
- Integers have a range of values, depending on the size of memory used.

The character data type

- The **char** primitive data type is simply a character, for example 'a'.
- This type:
  - represents symbolic information
  - gives each symbol a corresponding integer code
  - takes 16 bits of memory if you are using a single two-byte (16-bit) Unicode character.

> **Char** is an alphabet letter or symbol in the written form of a natural language. Python does not support characters.

The string data type

- A **string** variable is a sequence of **alphanumeric** characters and allowed symbols that are contained within quotation marks.
- "Hello world" is an example of a string.
- Strings can also be contained within single quotes.
- Strings are basically boxes used for storing text.
- A string:
  - represents a sequence of characters
  - is declared by the string keyword
  - has default value null (no value).
- Strings can be concatenated using the + operator.

> A **string** is a data type used to store a sequence of letters, symbols and/or numeric characters.
>
> **Alphanumeric** refers to alphabetic and numeric characters, and is used to describe the collection of Latin letters and Arabic numeric digits.

Floating-point types

- Floating-point numbers:
  - have a decimal point
  - represent **real** numbers
  - may be signed or unsigned
  - have a range of values and different precision depending on the memory used
  - can behave abnormally in calculations.

> A **real** number can have decimal or fractional parts.

> **Exam tip**
>
> Real numbers may also be described as float.

> **Exam tip**
>
> If you don't have time to write sentences, but you do know what to do, then just write bullet points.

The Boolean data type

- A **Boolean**:
  - is declared by the `bool` keyword
  - has two possible values: `true` or `false`
  - is useful in logical expressions
  - has a default value of `false`.

A **Boolean** expression is an expression that when evaluated is either `true` or `false`.

String manipulation

REVISED

- A string is simply a list of characters in order, where a character can be anything a user can type on the keyboard in a single keystroke.
- An empty string is a string that has 0 characters.
- Most code recognises as strings everything that is delimited by quotation marks (either " " or ' ').
- We can also manipulate strings using some built-in methods.
- The following pseudo-code can be used for manipulating strings.

String length

```
LEN(StringExp)
```

Example:

```
LEN('computer science')   # evaluates to 16
                          # (including space)
```

Position of a character

```
POSITION(StringExp, CharExp)
```

Example:

```
POSITION('computer science', 'm')   # evaluates to 2
# As with arrays, exam papers will make it clear
# whether indexing starts at 0 or 1.
# Here, 0 has been assumed.
```

Substring

```
SUBSTRING(IntExp, IntExp, StringExp)
```

The first parameter indicates the start position within the string, the second parameter indicates the final position within the string and the third parameter is the string itself.

Example:

```
SUBSTRING(2, 9, 'computer science')   # evaluates to
                                      # 'mputer s'
```

Concatenation

```
StringExp + StringExp
```

Example:

```
'computer' + 'science'   # evaluates to
                         # 'computerscience'
```

String and character conversion

Converting string to integer

```
STRING _ TO _ INT(StringExp)
```

Example:

```
STRING _ TO _ INT('16')  # evaluates to the integer 16
```

Converting string to real

```
STRING _ TO _ REAL(StringExp)
```

Example:

```
STRING _ TO _ REAL('16.3') # evaluates to the real
                           # number 16.3
```

Converting integer to string

```
INT _ TO _ STRING(IntExp)
```

Example:

```
INT _ TO _ STRING(16)   # evaluates to the string '16'
```

Converting real to string

```
REAL _ TO _ STRING(RealExp)
```

Example:

```
REAL _ TO _ STRING(16.3)   # evaluates to the string
                           # '16.3'
```

Converting character to character code

```
CHAR _ TO _ CODE(CharExp)
```

Example:

```
CHAR _ TO _ CODE('a')   # evaluates to 97 using ASCII/
                        # Unicode
```

Converting character code to character

```
CODE _ TO _ CHAR(IntExp)
```

Example:

```
CODE _ TO _ CHAR(97)   # evaluates to 'a' using ASCII/
                       # Unicode
```

Scope

- You will need to understand scope in order to effectively use subroutines, as local variables usually:
  - only exist while the subroutine is executing
  - are only accessible within the subroutine.
- A variable's scope consists of all the code blocks in which it is visible.
- A variable is considered visible if it can be accessed by statements within that code block.

Local scope

- **Local scope** is limited to the block where a variable is declared.
- A block is the body of a control structure, the body of a function, or a place such as the file or string containing the code where the variable is declared.
- Different subroutines can have local variables with the same names because the functions cannot access each other's local variables.

> A local variable is created inside a subroutine and cannot be accessed by statements that are outside the function – it has **local scope**.

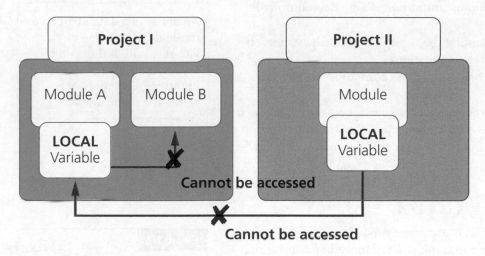

Global scope

- Global scope can be accessed from anywhere.
- In most programming languages variables are treated as global if not declared as local.
- In Python it is the opposite: variables are local if not declared as global.

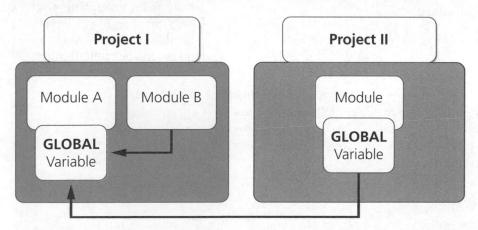

Why is it better to use local scope?

It is good programming style to use local variables whenever possible.

- It helps to avoid cluttering the global environment with unnecessary names.
- The **source code** is easier to understand when the scope of individual elements is limited.
- Subroutines can be more easily reused if their variables are all local.
- Global variables can be read or modified by any part of the program. A global variable can be accessed or set by any part of the program, and any rules regarding its use can easily be broken or forgotten.
- Global names are also available everywhere. You may unknowingly end up using a global variable when you think you are using a local variable.
- Testing your code is harder if you use global variables.

> The **source code** is the original program code; it is the part of software most computer users never see.

> **Exam tip**
>
> Leave any questions that you are unsure about for the end.

Arrays

REVISED

- In programming, one of the most important design decisions involves which data structure to use.
- **Arrays** and linked lists are among the most common data structures, and each is applicable in different situations.
- Arrays and linked lists are both designed to store multiple elements, most often of the same type.
- An array is an ordered arrangement of data elements that are accessed by referencing their location within the array; a linked list is a group of elements, each of which contains a pointer that points to the following element.

> An **array** is a data structure made up of a series of variables all of the same type, grouped under one identifier. Elements are accessed using an index.

One-dimensional arrays

- An array is a series of elements of the same type placed in contiguous memory locations that can be individually referenced by adding an index to a unique identifier.

- In pseudo-code you use the following syntax to initialise a one-dimensional array with a set of values:
  ```
  SET Array TO [<value>, ...]
  ```
  Example:
  ```
  SET ArrayValues TO [1, 2, 3, 4, 5]
  ```
- A one-dimensional array is a data structure that allows a list of items to be stored with the capability of accessing each item by pointing to its location (index) within the array.
- In pseudo-code you use the following syntax to assign a value to an element of a one-dimensional array:
  ```
  SET Array[index] TO <value>
  ```

  Example:
  ```
  SET ArrayClass[1] TO 'Steve'
  SET ArrayMarks[3] TO 66
  ```

> **Exam tip**
>
> Manage your time. The number of marks is important – normally one mark relates to about one minute. This is where you need to be strict on yourself; you **must** move on once you have spent enough time on a question or you won't be able to give the next question your full attention.

Two-dimensional arrays

- Two-dimensional arrays are a little more complex than the one-dimensional arrays, but really they are nothing more than an array of arrays; in other words, an array in one row and another in the next row.

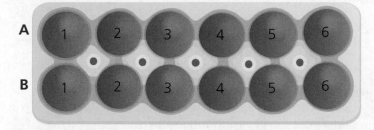

- The best way of understanding a two-dimensional array is to think of it as a way of holding and accessing information within a matrix or grid made up of rows and columns.

	0	1	2	3
0	A	B	C	D
1	E	F	G	H
2	I	J	K	L
3	M	N	O	P
4	Q	R	S	T

Exam tip

Read all the questions carefully before starting and quickly plan how much time to allocate to each.

- In pseudo-code you use the following syntax for a count-controlled loop that executes for each element of an array:

```
FOR EACH <id> FROM <expression> DO
    <command>
END FOREACH
```

Example:

```
SET wordsArray TO ['The', 'sky', 'is', 'blue']
SET Sentence to ''
FOR EACH Word FROM wordsArray DO
    SET Sentence TO Sentence & ' ' & Word
END FOREACH
```

- In pseudo-code you use the following syntax to assign a value to an element of a two-dimensional array:

```
SET Array [RowIndex, ColumnIndex] TO <value>
```

Example:

```
SET ArrayClassMarks[2,4] TO 33
```

Exam practice

1 In programming, what is a string? [4]

2 What will the following pseudo-code evaluate to?
```
LEN('Edexcel')
```
[1]

3 What are local variables? [2]

4 What are global variables? [2]

5 What will the following pseudo-code evaluate to?
```
'programming' + 'is' + 'cool'
```
[1]

6 What will the following pseudo-code do?
```
INT _ TO _ STRING(16)
```
[1]

7 In mathematics, which of the following are integers?
8, 5, 103, −1.33, $1\frac{3}{4}$, 98, 3.14, 1, 500.45, −9, 3, 5 [7]

8 Give two reasons why the integer data type would be used in programming rather than using the real data type. [1]

9 What is a real data type? [2]

10 What will the following pseudo-code do?
```
STRING _ TO _ REAL('1.3')
```
[1]

11 What will the following pseudo-code do?
```
STRING _ TO _ INT('16')
```
[1]

12 Write the pseudo-code to create a one-dimensional array with the following numbers:
2, 3, 5, 7, 11, 13 [1]

13 Arrays are the best data structures for: [1]
   a) relatively permanent collections of data
   b) when the size of the structure and the data in the structure are constantly changing
   c) both of the above situations
   d) none of the above situations.

14 Write the pseudo-code to change the number 13 to 17, in the array in question 12. [1]

15 Explain, using an example, the term 'one-dimensional array'. [1]

16 Explain the difference between one- and two-dimensional arrays. [2]

17 Why is the index of the first element in an array often 0 not 1? [1]

18 Explain why the elements of an array are stored successively in memory. [1]

19 Write the pseudo-code to create a two-dimensional array with the following numbers:
1, 2, 3
2, 4, 6
3, 6, 9
4, 8, 12 [1]

20 Given the array shown below, and the fact the index of the first element is 1, what number will
`tables[3][1]` equate to? [1]
```
tables = [[1,  2,  3],
          [2,  4,  6],
          [9,  6,  9],
          [4,  8,  12]]
```

Answers on p. 116

ANSWERS CHECKED ☐

2.4 Input/output

Input and output

REVISED ☐

This is how we show an input from a keyboard and output to a screen in our code:

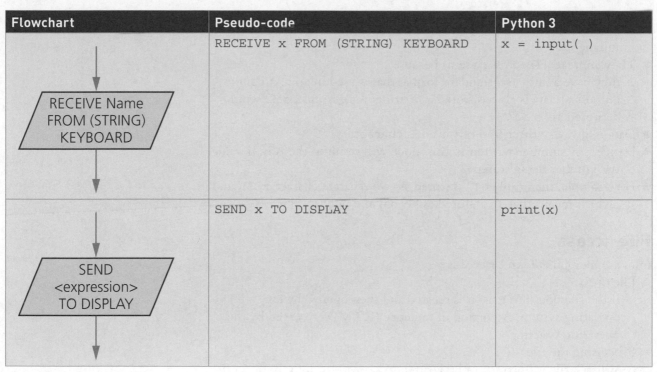

Flowchart	Pseudo-code	Python 3
RECEIVE Name FROM (STRING) KEYBOARD	`RECEIVE x FROM (STRING) KEYBOARD`	`x = input( )`
SEND <expression> TO DISPLAY	`SEND x TO DISPLAY`	`print(x)`

In pseudo-code you use the following syntax to receive data from a device:

```
RECEIVE <identifier> FROM (type) <device>
```

Examples:

```
RECEIVE Name FROM (STRING) KEYBOARD
RECEIVE LengthOfJourney FROM (INTEGER) CARD _
READER
RECEIVE YesNo FROM (CHARACTER) CARD _ READER
```

In pseudo-code you use the following syntax to send output to the screen:

```
SEND <expression> TO DISPLAY
```

Example:

```
SEND 'Have a good day.' TO DISPLAY
```

Reading and writing to an external file

- A file is a permanent way to store data.
- Three types of file can be used for storing data:
  - sequential
  - random
  - binary.
- Sequential files are useful for:
  - storing text
  - easy implementation in programs
  - where real-time editing of the file is not required.
- Random file structures are useful for:
  - files that require real-time editing
  - storing records.
- Binary files are useful for:
  - storing numbers, programs and images
  - where no defined file structure is present.

Sequential files

- Sequential files are stored like a one-dimensional array but they are read from start to finish and so cannot be read from and written to simultaneously.
- They are readable across systems because:
  - they have a universal standard format that is used in all text editors
  - numerical data is always stored as a string; for example, 5.32 would be stored as "5.32".
- Data is always written and retrieved as **characters**.
- Hence, any number written in this mode will result in the ASCII value of the number being stored.
- For example, the number 17 is stored as two separate characters, '1' and '7', which means that 17 is stored as [49 55] and not as [17].

File access

Files are manipulated in three stages:

- File open
  - If the file does not exist it is created and then opened by the operating system. A portion of memory (RAM) is reserved by the operating system.
- Processing the file
  - When a file is open it can be written to or read from (or both, in the case of random and binary files).
  - Writing to a file will save it to backing store.
- Closing a file
  - When a file has been opened and processed it must then be closed. The operating system will then release the memory.

In pseudo-code you use the following syntax to read in a record from a file and assign it to a variable:

```
READ <file> <record>
```

Example:

```
READ MyFile.doc Record
```

Data validation

- The following **validation** checks are examples of simple data validation routines:
  - checking if an entered string has a minimum length
  - checking if a string is empty
  - checking if data entered lies within a given range (e.g. between 1 and 10).
- Validation is an automatic check performed by a computer to ensure that entered data is sensible/feasible. It does not check the **accuracy** of the data entered.
- Why use validation?
  - A program could crash if incorrect data is input by a user.
  - The code may also produce incorrect results when processing the data.

> **Validation** is the process of checking data as it is input to ensure that it is sensible; it does not check that it is correct.

The most common validation checks are:

Type of check	Explanation
Length check	Checks than an entered data value is no longer than a set number of characters. For example, checks that the data isn't too long or too short.
Presence check	Checks that some data has been entered into a field.
Range check	For example, a user of a computer system is likely to be aged between 3 and 110. The computer can be programmed only to accept age values between 3 and 110. However, this does not guarantee that the number typed in is correct. For example, the user could be 5 years of age but say that they are 16.
Type check	Checks that the value of data is of a particular type, for example that age data is numeric.
Format check	A format check is more advanced than a type check; for example, it can be used to check a postcode format.

- There are a number of other validation types that can be used to check the data that is being entered:
  - Cardinality check: checks that a record has a valid number of related records.
  - Check digit: the last one or two digits in a data field are used to check that the other digits are correct.
  - Consistency check: checks fields to ensure that data in these fields corresponds. For example, If Title = 'Mr.' then Gender = 'M'.
  - Spell check: looks up words in a dictionary or array of known words.

Validating the presence of data

One common error is no data in a field where data is required. For example, id is frequently required, as is name. A pseudo-code example testing for the presence of a name is shown below:

```
IF LEN(name) = 0 THEN    #invalid is a variable set
#when the string contains 0 characters
    SEND 'missing name' TO DISPLAY
    invalid = TRUE
END IF
```

Validating data type

Often, non-numeric data is put into a numeric field. However, you can validate for character data in a character field. Assume that myNumber is a numeric field and that you want to make sure that no non-numeric data is entered in the field:

```
invalid = FALSE
IF NOT is_numeric(myNumber) THEN
    SEND 'non-numeric data in myNumber' TO DISPLAY
    invalid = TRUE
END IF
```

Range checks

We can use similar code for a range check. Say we want to limit the maximum age someone can enter:

```
input = input('Please provide your age: ')
input = int(input)  # we must convert the user
                    # input to an integer
if input > 120 print('Error! You cannot be that old!')
END IF
```

Or the minimum age:

```
input = input('Please provide your age: ')
input = int(input)
if input < 6 print('Error! You cannot be that young!')
```

Exam practice

1 Briefly describe an exported sequential text file. [6]
2 Briefly explain the difference between a sequential file and a random access file. [6]

Answers on p. 116

ANSWERS CHECKED

2.5 Operators

Specification references

You must be able to:

2.5.1 demonstrate an understanding of the purpose of, and how to use, arithmetic operators (add, subtract, divide, multiply, modulus, integer division)

2.5.2 demonstrate an understanding of the purpose of, and how to use, relational operators (equal to, less than, greater than, not equal to, less than or equal to, greater than or equal to)

2.5.3 demonstrate an understanding of the purpose of, and how to use, logic operators (AND, OR, NOT)

Algorithms

REVISED

- The study of **algorithms** did not start with the invention of computers – adding two numbers together is a mathematical problem.
- When the term 'algorithm' is used in mathematics, it refers to a set of steps used to solve a mathematical problem.

> An **algorithm** is simply a set of steps that defines how a task is performed. It is a sequence of steps and decisions to solve a problem.

The algorithms for performing long division or multiplication are good examples. If you were carrying out a long division for 52 divided by 3, you would have the following specific sequence of steps and their outcomes:

- How many times does 3 go into 52?
  - The answer is 17 ($3 \times 17 = 51$).
- How many are left over?
  - The answer is 1.
- How many times does 3 go into 10?
  - The answer is 3 with 1 left over.

And, of course, the answer becomes 17.3333333.

The step-by-step process used to do the long division is called a long division algorithm. Algorithms are used a lot in mathematics, especially in algebra.

Differences

There are some important differences that you must understand:

Mathematics	Computer science
The following instructions are the same in mathematics: $A = B$ $B = A$ In mathematics both these instructions would express that A and B are equal, so they have the same purpose.	In computer science, = is used for assignment, so A = B copies the value of B into A, whereas B = A copies the value of A into B.
In mathematics we work with relations. The relation $B = A + 1$ means that it is true all the time.	In computer science we work with assignments. We can have: A = 5 B = A + 1 A = 3 The relation B = A + 1 is true only after the second instruction and before the third one. After the third one A is 3, but B is still 6.

Mathematics	Computer science
The instruction $A = A + 3$ is false in mathematics. It cannot exist.	In computer science $A = A + 3$ means: the new value of A is equal to the old one plus three.
The instruction $A + 6 = 3$ is allowed in mathematics (it is an equation).	$A + 6 = 3$ has no meaning in computer science, where the = is used for assignment. The left side must then be a variable, so we would have to say $three = A + 6$. In some languages we could use the following to see if they are equal: $A + 6 == 3$

Operators

REVISED

In order to program you will need to understand the syntax for mathematical operators. The mathematical operators used in pseudo-code are:

Symbol	Description
+	add
–	subtract
/	divide
*	multiply
^	exponent
DIV	integer division
MOD	modulo

The relational operators used in pseudo-code are:

Symbol	Description
=	equal to
<>	not equal to
>	greater than
>=	greater than or equal to
<	less than
<=	less than or equal to

> **Exam tip**
>
> Remember to read all the questions carefully. The stress of the examination can cause you to misread a question.

> **Exam tip**
>
> Remember, the exams are not designed to trick you. Convince yourself that you know how to answer exam questions and you're almost there.

Division

- Integer division including remainders is usually a two-stage process and uses modular arithmetic: e.g. the calculation 11/2 would generate the following values:
  - Integer division: the integer quotient of 11 divided by 2 (11 DIV 2) = 5
  - Remainder: the remainder when 11 is divided by 2 (11 MOD 2) = 1
- Standard use using brackets to make precedence obvious.
- The / symbol is used instead of ÷ for division (for integer division use DIV.)

Boolean

The **Boolean** operations used in pseudo-code are:

Symbol	Description
AND	Returns true if **both** conditions are true.
OR	Returns true if **any** of the conditions are true.
NOT	Reverses the outcome of the expression; true becomes false, false becomes true.

A **Boolean** expression is an expression that when evaluated is either true or false.

- The AND operator ensures that all the conditions are true before returning a value.
  - ○ `BoolExp AND BoolExp`
  - ○ Example: `(3 = 3) AND (3 ≤ 4)`
- The OR operator requires at least one of the specified conditions to be true. In searches, you use OR to retrieve records or pages that contain **either** of two or more terms. The OR operator is generally used to assess similar, equivalent or synonymous conditions.
  - ○ `BoolExp OR BoolExp`
  - ○ Example: `(x < 1) OR (x > 9)`
- The NOT operator inverts the value of a Boolean expression. Thus, if b is true, NOT b is false. If b is false, NOT b is true.
  - ○ `NOT BoolExp`
  - ○ Example: `NOT (another _ go = FALSE)`

Condition-controlled iteration

REVISED

Repeat–until

Repeat the statements until the Boolean expression is true.

```
REPEAT
    # statements here
UNTIL BoolExp
```

Example:

```
a = 1
REPEAT
    SEND a TO DISPLAY
    a = a + 1
UNTIL a = 4
# will output 1, 2, 3
```

While

While the Boolean expression is true, repeat the statements.

```
WHILE BoolExp
    # statements here
END WHILE
```

Example:

```
a = 1
WHILE a < 4
    SEND a TO DISPLAY
    a = a + 1
END WHILE
# will output 1, 2, 3
```

Exam practice

1 Write pseudo-code such that the user inputs the dimensions of a rectangle, and the perimeter and area of the rectangle are shown on the computer screen. [6]

2 Write the pseudo-code to ask the user to input a number and output to the screen whether it is an odd or even number. [6]

3 Complete the chart shown by adding the descriptions. One has been done for you. [5]

Operator	Description
>	greater than
<	
=	
>=	
<=	
!=	

4 Write pseudo-code such that the user inputs the length of the side of a square, and its area is printed. Produce an error message if the length entered by the user is negative. [5]

5 Write pseudo-code such that the user inputs three numbers and the following is shown on the screen: either 'all three equal' or 'not all equal'. [5]

6 Write pseudo-code such that the user inputs three numbers and the largest is shown on the screen. [6]

7 The basic operations performed by a computer are: [1]
   a) arithmetic operation
   b) logical operation
   c) storage and relational operations
   d) all the above.

8 Fill in the missing descriptions in the table below. [4]

Operator	Description
MOD	
–	
*	
DIV	

9 Write pseudo-code to calculate the result of integer division of 9 by 5. [1]

10 Write pseudo-code to calculate the remainder of integer division of 9 by 5. [1]

Answers on pp. 116–17

ANSWERS CHECKED ☐

2.6 Subprograms

Specification references

You must be able to:

2.6.1 demonstrate an understanding of the benefits of using subprograms and write code that uses user-written and pre-existing (built-in, library) subprograms

2.6.2 demonstrate an understanding of the concept of passing data into and out of subprograms (procedures, functions)

2.6.3 be able to create subprograms that use parameters

Structured programming

REVISED

- Structured programming is sometimes also called modular programming.
- It is important that structured programming uses clear, well-documented interfaces such as local variables and parameters alongside clearly defined return values.
- Defined functions are coded in a separate module. This means that modules can be reused in other programs.
- After a module has been tested individually, it is then integrated with other modules into the overall program structure. Structured programs use looping constructs such as `for`, `until` and `while`.
- Each basic subroutine of a program should perform a simple task.
- A subtask could require a single unit, or a combination of units.
- Generally speaking, a function returns a value and can be included within an expression; a procedure doesn't.
- The benefits of modular programming are:
  - It makes the coding so much easier.
  - Once written, modules can be checked individually and then placed in the correct order within the program.
  - Some tasks are quite generic; for example, you may need to perform a particular mathematical operation within your code.
- To avoid unnecessary work, all programming languages have predefined modules that can be called. It is possible to 'call' any module.
- When a module is called, the name for this is a **subroutine** or **procedure**.
- A procedure is a special kind of module that performs a task or set of tasks that can be added to another program as a subtask.

> **Exam tip**
>
> The terms 'arguments' and 'parameters' are sometimes used, but 'parameter' can be used to refer to both of these.

> A **subroutine** is a sequence of instructions that is set up to perform a frequently performed task. It is a computer program contained within another program. It operates semi-independently of the main program. A subroutine is a named 'out of line' block of code that may be executed (called) by simply writing its name in a program statement.
>
> **Procedures** are collections of statements that define what happens to the parameters. A procedure is a subroutine that does not return values.

In pseudo-code you use the following syntax to define a procedure:

```
PROCEDURE <id> (<parameter>, ...)
BEGIN PROCEDURE
    <command>
END PROCEDURE
```

Example:

```
PROCEDURE CalculateAverage(Mark1, Mark2, Mark3)
BEGIN PROCEDURE
    SET Avg TO (Mark1 + Mark2 + Mark3)/3
END PROCEDURE
```

In pseudo-code you use the following syntax to define a function:

```
FUNCTION <id> (<parameter>, ...)
BEGIN FUNCTION
    <command>
    RETURN <expression>
END FUNCTION
```

Example:

```
FUNCTION myMarks (Mark1, Mark2, Mark3)
BEGIN FUNCTION
    SET Total TO Mark1 + Mark2 + Mark3
    RETURN Total
END FUNCTION
```

In pseudo-code you use the following syntax to call a procedure or a function:

```
<id>(<parameter>, ...)
```

Example:

```
Add(firstNumber, secondNumber)
```

Subroutine return value:

```
RETURN Exp
```

Example:

```
SUBROUTINE add(a, b)
    result = a + b
    RETURN result
END SUBROUTINE
```

Calling a subroutine:

```
Identifier(parameters)
```

Example:

```
show _ add(2, 3)
answer = add(2, 3)
```

The concept of subroutines

REVISED

- You need to break sections of code into separate logical units.
- The code associated with accomplishing each task should be separated from the code that accomplishes other tasks.
- These actions are referred to as events and are one way of breaking up code into smaller, more logical, units.
- Another way to break up an application is by using either **functions** or subroutines.

> A **function** is a group of statements that exist within a program for the purpose of performing a specific task. In computer programming a function is a subprogram; given a particular set of argument values, the function returns a unique result.

The advantages of using subroutines

- Programs are made more readable by breaking large amounts of code into smaller, more concise, parts.
- By breaking code into functions and subroutines, code can be written once and reused often.
- This reduces the size of the application and reduces **debugging** time.
- Functions and subroutines operate similarly, but they have one key difference:
  - A function is used when a value is returned to the calling routine.
  - A subroutine is used when a desired task is needed, but no value is returned.

> The process of testing a program for errors during its execution is a cyclic activity called **debugging**.

Parameters

- Parameters pass data within programs.
- They are the names of the information that we want to use in a function or procedure.
- They allow us to pass information or instructions into functions and procedures.
- They are useful when we are using number information.
- Parameter values passed in are called **arguments**.
- Subroutines return values to the calling routine.
- Parameter passing is the mechanism used to pass parameters to a procedure (subroutine) or function.
- The most common methods are to pass the value of the actual parameter, which is referred to as 'call by value'.
- It is also possible to pass the address of the memory location where the actual parameter is stored; this is referred to as 'call by reference'.

> An **argument** is any piece of data that is passed into a function when the function is called.

Exam practice

1 What is a function? [2]
2 What is a user-defined function and why would they be used? [4]
3 What do you mean by a calling function? [2]
4 What is an argument? [1]
5 What are actual parameters? [2]
6 What are formal parameters? [2]
7 How is a function invoked? [2]
8 State the three different structured programming constructs. [3]
9 What is structured programming? [2]
10 Give two characteristics of structured programming. [2]
11 Give two advantages of structured programming. [2]
12 State the four main advantages of structured programming. [4]
13 What is a structure? [1]
14 What is meant by an array of structures? [1]
15 Write pseudo-code to output the numbers 1 to 50 inclusive using a WHILE loop. [5]
16 Write pseudo-code to output the numbers 1 to 60 inclusive with a FOR loop. [5]
17 Write pseudo-code to ask the user to input two values into variables for start and finish, then print the integers from start to finish inclusive using a FOR loop. [5]
18 Write pseudo-code to ask the user to input two values into variables for start and finish, then print the integers from start to finish inclusive using a FOR loop, but if start is bigger than finish output an error message instead! [8]

Answers on pp. 117–18

ANSWERS CHECKED

3.1 Binary

Specification references

You must be able to:

3.1.1 demonstrate an understanding of the use of binary in computers to represent data (numbers, text, sound, graphics) and program instructions

3.1.2 demonstrate an understanding of how computers represent and manipulate numbers (unsigned integers, signed integers – sign and magnitude, two's complement)

3.1.3 convert between binary and denary whole numbers (0–255)

3.1.4 demonstrate an understanding of how to perform binary arithmetic (add; logical and arithmetic shifts) and the concept of overflow

3.1.5 demonstrate an understanding of why hexadecimal notation is used and be able to convert between hexadecimal and binary

Binary numbers

Everything a computer does is based on **binary** numbers, ones and zeros. 1 means 'on' and 0 means 'off'.

> **Binary** is a system of numbers using only the two digits 0 and 1 (also called the base 2 system), unlike the decimal (or denary) system in everyday use that uses 0 to 9 (base 10). All data that is stored in a computer is converted to binary.

| On | On | Off | On | Off | Off |

- Rather than giving a light just one score, we give the different lights in the sequence different scores.
- The first light is 32, the second 16, then 8, 4, 2, 1.
- The value of those six bulbs (called a point value) would be: 32 + 16 + 0 + 4 + 0 + 0 (remember, we only give points if they're turned on!), which adds up to 52.
- So, we would say the sequence of lights is worth 52.
- But we would write it as 110100.

Converting decimal to binary numbers

First, consider the decimal digits 0–9.

Decimal number	How we convert	Binary number
0	We start at 0 for the number of bits required. Here we have 7 bits.	0000000
1	Then we add a 1 on the right.	0000001
2	As we already have a 1 on the right it changes back to 0 again, but we carry a 1 one place in.	0000010
3	Now we add a 1 on the right again as it is a 0.	0000011
4	We add 1 to the number on the right but that digit is already a 1 so it goes back to 0 and 1 is added to the *next position* on the left, but it is also a 1 so it becomes a zero and we carry the 1 one place to the left.	0000100

Decimal number	How we convert	Binary number
5	Now we add a 1 on the right again as it is a 0.	0000101
6	As we want to add a 1 to the right and it is already a 1 we make it a 0 and move the 1 up one place to the left.	0000110
7	Now we add a 1 on the right again as it is a 0.	0000111
8	Start back at 0 again (for all three digits), and a 1 is carried to the left.	0001000
9	And so on ...	0001001

To convert from decimal numbers to binary we divide the number successively by 2 and print the remainder in reverse order. So, if we have a decimal number of 51 we can work out its binary number as follows:

Number divided by 2		Remainder
$\frac{51}{2}$	25	1
$\frac{25}{2}$	12	1
$\frac{12}{2}$	6	0
$\frac{6}{2}$	3	0
$\frac{3}{2}$	1	1
$\frac{1}{2}$	0	1

Answer: 110011

Binary addition

- Adding binary numbers is relatively simple:
  - $0 + 0 = 0$
  - $1 + 0 = 1$
  - $0 + 1 = 1$
  - $1 + 1 = 0$ carry 1
  - $1 + 1 + 1 = 1$ carry 1
- To add two binary numbers you first align the numbers you wish to add as you would if you were adding decimal numbers.

```
0 1 1 1
1 1 1 0
```

- You then add the two numbers in the far right column, again as you would with decimal numbers.

```
  0 1 1 1
  1 1 1 0
  -------
        1
```

- Add the numbers following the rules of binary addition ($1 + 0 = 1$, $0 + 0 = 0$) unless both numbers are a 1. If they are both 1, write 0 below and carry a 1 to the next column. (Remember, it is not 'ten' but 'one zero'.)

```
  0 1 1 1
  1 1 1 0
  -------
      0 1
```

- Move on to the next column to the left. We use the rule 1 + 1 + 1 = 1 carry 1.

```
  0 1 1 1
  1 1 1 0
  ───────
    1 0 1
```

- We start on the right and move across the columns to the left. If there are no more columns, we add a new one.

```
    0 1 1 1
    1 1 1 0
  ─────────
  1 0 1 0 1
```

- Remember that 1 + 1 = 10 and 1 + 1 + 1 = 11. Always remember to carry the 1. If we want to add three binary numbers this is achieved in exactly same way. When we add three numbers the rule is that 1 + 1 + 1 + carry 1 = 100.

```
      1 1 0 1
      1 0 1 1
      1 1 0 1
  ───────────
  1 0 0 1 0 1
```

  - Rightmost column = 1 + 1 + 1 so we have 1 and need to also carry 1 to the next column.
  - Next column = 0 + 1 + 0 but we also have the 1 carried so 0 and we carry 1 again to the next column.
  - Next column = 1 + 0 + 1 + the 1 that was carried so the answer is 1 with a carry of 1.
  - In the fourth column we have 1 + 1 + 1 with a carry of 1 as well. Adding four 1s results in a 0 in this column with a 1 carried two columns to the left.
  - Two new columns need to be created for the 1 to be carried across by two columns.
  - The answer: 100101.

Binary shift

- If we shift the decimal point in a decimal number to the right, it multiplies the number by 10. So 1.2 would become 12. If we move the point two places it would become 120. This is because we use a base 10 numbering system.
- Binary uses a base 2 system and therefore a **shift** one place to the left in a binary number is the same as multiplying by 2:

> Binary **shifts** can be used to perform simple multiplication/division by powers of 2.

Decimal	128	64	32	16	8	4	2	1
Input	0	0	1	0	0	1	0	1
Result	0	1	0	0	1	0	1	0

- A left shift of 2 places is the same as multiplying by 4:

Decimal	128	64	32	16	8	4	2	1
Input	0	0	1	0	0	1	0	1
Result	1	0	0	1	0	1	0	0

- A left shift of 3 places is the same as multiplying by 8:

Decimal	256	128	64	32	16	8	4	2	1
Input	0	0	0	1	0	0	1	0	1
Result	1	0	0	1	0	1	0	0	0

- In general, shifting N places left is the same as multiplying by 2 to the power N (written as 2^N).
- If we shift to the right 1 place this is the same as dividing by 2.

Decimal	256	128	64	32	16	8	4	2	1
Input	0	0	1	0	0	1	0	1	0
Result	0	0	0	1	0	0	1	0	1

Hexadecimal numbers

- Computers can use what are called **hexadecimal** numbers. There are 16 hexadecimal digits:

Decimal	0	1	2	3	4	5	6	7	8	9	10	11	12	13	14	15
Hexadecimal:	0	1	2	3	4	5	6	7	8	9	A	B	C	D	E	F

- Hexadecimal numbers are the same as decimal up to 9:

Decimal	Hexadecimal	Binary
0	0	0000
1	1	0001
2	2	0010
3	3	0011
4	4	0100
5	5	0101
6	6	0110
7	7	0111
8	8	1000
9	9	1001
10	A	1010
11	B	1011
12	C	1100
13	D	1101
14	E	1110
15	F	1111

The word **hexadecimal** (or hex for short) means 'based on 16', from the Greek hexa (six) and Latin decima (a tenth part).

Decimals to hexadecimal

Converting decimal numbers to hexadecimal numbers is much harder than converting decimals to binary numbers. We always work backwards to convert these numbers.

Suppose we want to convert the decimal number 1128 to hexadecimal:

What to do	Division	Integer	Remainder (in hexadecimal)
Start by dividing the number by 16, that is $\frac{1128}{16}$. 1128 divided by 16 is 70.5. So the integer division result is 70; record this in the Integer column. The remainder is (70.5 – 70) = 0.5. This is then multiplied by 16, giving a result of 8. Record this in the Remainder column.	$\frac{1128}{16}$	70	8
Now divide the result number by 16: $\frac{70}{16}$ = 4.375. So the integer division result is 4. The remainder, 0.375, is multiplied by 16, which is 6.	$\frac{70}{16}$	4	6
The next stage is $\frac{4}{16}$ = 0.25. The integer division result is 0. The remainder, 0.25, is multiplied by 16, which is 4.	$\frac{4}{16}$	0	4
Stop because the result is already 0 (0 divided by 16 will always be 0). We now have the hexadecimal equivalent of the decimal number 1128 by working up from the bottom of our remainder column: 468.			

Hexadecimal to decimal

Suppose that the number 1128 was a hexadecimal number and not a decimal number, and we wanted to find its decimal equivalent. This would be calculated as follows:

- The last number is 8. It represents $8 \times (16^0)$ which equals 8.
- The next number is 2. This represents $2 \times (16^1)$ = 32.
- The next number is 1. This will be $1 \times (16^2)$ = 256.
- And lastly $1 \times (16^3)$ = 4096.
- If we add the totals together, 1128 in hexadecimal = 4392 in denary.

Exam practice

1 Complete the binary addition chart shown below. One entry has been done for you. Your answer should be shown as an eight-bit number. [4]

Addition	Answer
101 + 11 =	00001000
111 + 111 =	
1010 + 1010 =	
11101 + 1010 =	
11111 + 11111 =	

2 A number system that has two different symbols to represent any quantity is known as [1]
   a) binary   b) octal   c) decimal   d) hexadecimal
3 A number system that has ten different symbols to represent any quantity is known as [1]
   a) binary   b) octal   c) decimal   d) hexadecimal
4 A number system that has eight different symbols to represent any quantity is known as [1]
   a) binary   b) octal   c) decimal   d) hexadecimal
5 A number system that has 16 different symbols to represent any quantity is known as [1]
   a) binary   b) octal   c) decimal   d) hexadecimal
6 The least significant bit of the binary number equivalent to any odd decimal number is [1]
   a) 0   b) 1   c) 1 or 0   d) 3

Answers on p. 118

ANSWERS CHECKED

3.2 Data representation

Specification references

You must be able to:

3.2.1 demonstrate an understanding of how computers encode characters using ASCII

3.2.2 demonstrate an understanding of how bitmap images are represented in binary (pixels, resolution, colour depth)

3.2.3 demonstrate an understanding of how sound, an analogue signal, is represented in binary

3.2.4 demonstrate an understanding of the limitations of binary representations of data (sampling frequency, resolution) when constrained by the number of available bits

Characters

REVISED

ASCII

- **ASCII** stands for American Standard Code for Information Interchange.
- Computers can only understand numbers, so an ASCII code is the numerical representation of characters such as 'a', 'z', '@' or even an action of some sort.
- The original ASCII only uses 7-bit numbers to represent the letters, numerals and common punctuation used in the English language.
- As there are two possibilities per bit, we have $2^7 = 128$ possible values that can be represented, from 0 to 127 inclusive. Remember, 0 is also a reference so we have 128 possible values to store our characters.
- Each of those 128 values is assigned to a character:

> **ASCII** (American Standard Code for Information Interchange) is a 7-bit system to code the character set on a computer.

	0000	0001	0010	0011	0100	0101	0110	0111
0000	NULL	DLE		0	@	P	`	p
0001	SOH	DC1	!	1	A	Q	a	q
0010	STX	DC2	"	2	B	R	b	r
0011	ETX	DC3	#	3	C	S	c	s
0100	EDT	DC4	$	4	D	T	d	t
0101	ENQ	NAK	%	5	E	U	e	u
0110	ACK	SYN	&	6	F	V	f	v
0111	BEL	ETB	'	7	G	W	g	w
1000	BS	CAN	(	8	H	X	h	x
1001	HT	EM	)	9	I	Y	i	y
1010	LF	SUB	*	:	J	Z	j	z
1011	VT	ESC	+	;	K	[	k	{
1100	FF	FS	,	<	L	\	l	|
1101	GR	GS	-	=	M	]	m	}
1110	SO	RS	.	>	N	^	n	~
1111	SI	US	/	?	O	_	o	DEL

- For example, in ASCII the number 65 represents an upper-case letter 'A' and 61 represents an equals sign. So if the output sent to a display receives an ASCII value of 65, it displays an upper-case letter A on the screen.
- There is no real reason that A has to be character number 65, that's just the number the developers working on telegraph systems chose when ASCII was first developed.
- In ASCII, codes run sequentially so ASCII 'A' is coded as 65, 'B' as 66, and so on, meaning that the codes for the other capital letters can be calculated once the code for 'A' is known. This pattern also applies to other groupings such as lower-case letters and digits.
- If we wanted to translate 'Hello' into ASCII it would look like this:

ASCII	01001000	01100101	01101100	01101100	01101111
Text	H	e	l	l	o

Extended ASCII

- ASCII works fine for English strings such as 'Hello World', but what if we want to store a German string such as 'Es gefällt mir nicht' (translates as: I do not like it)?
- So it was decided that if ASCII was made into an 8-bit code rather than 7, it could store another 128 values. This system is called extended ASCII.
- The problem was that different groups used the same initial ASCII characters, but came up with different extended ASCII character set numbers. For example, in the Western Europe extended ASCII character set, number 224 represents a lower-case letter A with a grave accent. But in Eastern Europe the same number represents a lower-case letter R with an acute accent.
- Added to this, 256 characters is no use in languages like Chinese or Japanese, where there are literally thousands of characters in common use.

The Unicode character set

- Although originally designed for 16 bits, the latest version of **Unicode** stores each character with 32 bits. Unicode can also use 8 bits.
- It presently contains over 110,000 characters and has space for 1,114,111 different values that can be used for characters, so at present only around 10% are used.
- Unicode uses the same codes as ASCII up to 127.
- The chart shows just a few of the foreign language characters supported.

> **Unicode** is a universal code used by computers to represent thousands of symbols and text characters. It uses a system of up to 32 bits to code the character set of a computer (usually 16-bit or 32-bit versions).

Code (Hex)	Character	Source
0041	A	English (Latin)
042F	Я	Russian (Cyrillic)
262F	☯	Symbols
03A3	Σ	Greek
211E	℞	Letter-like symbols
21CC	⇌	Arrows
28FF	⣿	Braille
2EDD	⻝	Chinese/Japanese/Korean (Common)

Bitmaps

- A **bitmap** image stores each individual **pixel**.
- First you need to understand black and white images. 0 is stored for a white pixel, 1 is stored for a black pixel. Each black and white pixel takes up 1 bit of storage.
- An example would be:

0	0	1	1	1	1	0	0
0	1	0	0	0	0	1	0
0	1	0	0	0	0	1	0
1	0	1	0	0	1	0	1
0	1	0	0	0	0	1	0
0	1	0	1	1	0	1	0
0	0	1	0	0	1	0	0
0	0	0	1	1	0	0	0

> A **bitmap** is a graphical image represented as an array of brightness values. For example, in a black and white image 0 represents white and 1 represents black.
>
> **Pixels** are the dots that make a graphical image on screen. They are the smallest element of an image.

- This would create the following image:

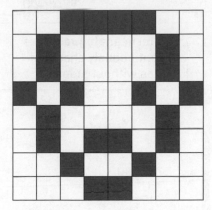

Resolution

- **Resolution** is the name we use for the number of pixels that the image is made up of. It relates to the number of pixels displayed on the screen.
- A higher resolution gives a clearer and more detailed picture but uses more pixels and hence takes up more memory.

> The **resolution** is the number of pixels or dots, for example ppi (pixels per inch), often referred to as dpi (dots per inch).

Greyscale images

- A greyscale (black and white) image uses one **byte** per pixel (a byte being eight **bits**).
- Eight bits means that a byte can store up to 256 levels of information.
- We can therefore store up to 256 levels of brightness per pixel – which gives us what is called '8–bit greyscale'.

> A **byte** is a group of binary (0 or 1) digits made up of eight bits.
>
> A single binary digit (like 0 or 1) is called a **bit**. For example, 11010 is five bits long. The word 'bit' is made up from the words 'binary digit'.

Calculating storage requirements

- If we need to calculate the storage requirements of a black and white bitmap image, we multiply the number of pixels wide by the number of pixels high.
- The answer will give us the number of bits.
- We then convert the number into an appropriate unit (kilobytes/ megabytes).

A black and white image is 800 pixels by 900 pixels. Calculate the storage requirements and express the answer in appropriate units.

Step 1: length × breadth

800 × 900 = 720,000 bits

Step 2: Convert into appropriate units

720,000/8 = 90,000 bytes

90,000 bytes/1000 = 90 kb

Exam tip

You will only need to use colour depth and number of pixels within your calculations.

- VDUs (video display units) display pictures by dividing the display screen into thousands (or millions) of pixels, arranged into rows and columns.
- The size of an image is expressed directly as the width of the image in pixels by the height of the image in pixels using the notation width × height.
- Colour depth is the number of bits used to represent each pixel.
  - Size in bits = W × H × D
  - Size in bytes = W × H × D/8
  - W = image width, H = image height, D = colour depth in bits.

Sound

REVISED

- Original sound is **analogue**, it's how our ears work.
- To turn this sound into something a computer can handle we need to create a digital sound wave.

The term **analogue** refers to continuously changing values without steps.

Original analogue sound wave

Digitised sound wave

- In analogue recordings, the machine is constantly recording any sound or noise that is coming through the microphones.
- In digital recording you don't have a constant recording, you have a series of **samples** or snapshots which are a measure of amplitude at a given point in time and are taken from the sound being recorded.

A **sample** is a point in time where a measurement of an analogue signal is taken (sampled). The unit of sample rate is 'samples per second'. This is often expressed in kilohertz (kHz).

Analogue to digital converter

- An analogue to digital converter constantly measures the amplitude (volume) of an incoming electrical voltage from a microphone or sound source.
- It then outputs these measurements as a long list of binary bytes: 101101001010001010010010010010101010101
- The sampling rate is the number of samples taken in a second and is usually measured in hertz (1 hertz = 1 sample per second).
- The sample resolution is the number of bits per sample.
- File size (bits) = rate × res × secs
  ○ rate = sampling rate
  ○ res = sample resolution
  ○ secs = number of seconds
- Given a bitmap representation, you will be expected to show the frequency and value pairs for each row:
  ○ For example, 0000011100000011 would become 5 0 3 1 6 0 2 1.

Sampling

- Bit depth defines the dynamic range of the sound – the amplitude (volume) of the waveform at each sample point.
- Quantisation is the name of the audio snapshot when it has to be rounded off to the nearest available digital value.
- Sample rates are measured in hertz (Hz) or thousands of hertz (kHz, kilohertz). For example, 44.1 kHz is equal to 44,100 samples of audio recorded every second.
- The sample rate you choose depends on what the audio is going to be used for. If you wanted to record a song to put on a CD you would usually use 44.1 kHz.

Calculating file sizes

- We can calculate sound file sizes based on the **sample rate** and the **sample resolution** using the following formula: File size (bits) = rate × res × secs
- If we want 30 seconds of mono sound, where the sample rate is 44,100 Hz and the sample resolution is 8 bits, we will have:

(44100 × 8 × 30)/(8 × 1000)
[divided by 8 as we have 8 bits in a byte and 1000 to get kB]

= 1323 kB

= 1.32 MB

- The size of 30 seconds of stereo sound would be:

(44100 × 8 × 2 × 30)/(8 × 1000)

= 2646 kB

= 2.6 MB

> The **sample rate** is the number of times the sound is sampled per second. It is measured in Hz (100 Hz is 100 samples per second).
>
> The **sample resolution** is the space available for each sample, measured in kilobits.

Bit rate

- Digital music files are measured by the amount of information they can play per second, usually measured in kbps, or kilobits per second. This is the amount of sound information presented to the listener every second.
- The bit rate is the number of bits per second.
- Sound files played over internet radio are 56 or 64 kbps, to allow faster transport over networks.
- The standard for near-CD quality is 128 kbps, and some files go up to 320 kbps.
- If we have a 30-second audio file sampled at a rate of 44.1 kHz and quantised using 8 bits, we can calculate its bit rate by: `bit rate = bitsPerSample × samplesPerSecond × number of channels`
- To get the file size we would simply multiply the bit rate by the duration (in seconds), and divide by 8 (to get from bits to bytes): `fileSize = (bitsPerSample × samplesPerSecond × channels × duration)/8`

Exam practice

1 A microphone is left on for 20 hours recording MP3 audio files. If an MP3 uses 1 MB in one minute, how much data will that be, expressed in GB? [2]

2 Describe the differences between analogue and digital recordings. [4]

3 What does ASCII stand for? [1]
   a) American Standard Code for Information Interchange
   b) American Scientific Code for International Interchange
   c) American Standard Code for Intelligence Interchange
   d) American Scientific Code for Information Interchange

4 The original ASCII code used __ bits of each byte, reserving the last bit for error checking. [1]
   a) 5   b) 6   c) 7   d) 8

5 What will the following pseudo-code do? [1]

   `CHAR_TO_CODE('a')`

6 What will the following pseudo-code do? [1]

   `CODE_TO_CHAR(97)`

7 What is the commonly used standard data code to represent alphabetical, numerical and punctuation characters used in electronic data processing systems? [1]
   a) ASCII
   b) ASCIII
   c) high-level language
   d) low-level language

8 What is the difference between ASCII and extended ASCII? [2]

9 What are the main advantages of Unicode over ASCII? [4]

10 Describe the differences between digital and analogue data. [6]

11 Which of the following require large amounts of a computer's memory? [1]
   a) imaging
   b) graphics
   c) voice
   d) all of the above

12 A true-colour image is 800 pixels by 900 pixels. Calculate the storage requirements and express the answer in appropriate units. A true-colour image uses 24 bits to represent RGB colours. [6]

13 You take a digital photograph which is 800 pixels by 600 pixels. Each pixel has its own red, green and blue values stored in 1 byte. How many bytes are required to store the whole image in RAM and how would this differ on a hard drive where it is stored as a JPEG file? [5]

Answers on p. 118

ANSWERS CHECKED

3.3 Data storage and compression

Specification references

You must be able to:

3.3.1 demonstrate an understanding of how to convert between the terms bit, nibble, byte, kilobyte (kB), megabyte (MB), gigabyte (GB), terabyte (TB)

3.3.2 demonstrate an understanding of the need for data compression and methods of compressing data (lossless, lossy), and that JPEG and MP3 are examples of lossy algorithms

3.3.3 demonstrate an understanding of how a lossless run-length encoding (RLE) algorithm works

3.3.4 demonstrate an understanding that file storage is measured in bytes and be able to calculate file sizes

Key concepts

REVISED

- A **bit** has a value of either 1 or 0 (on or off). It is the fundamental unit of information.
- A nibble is four bits.
- A **byte** is group of eight bits.
- Large numbers of bytes can be described using prefixes:
  - kilo: 1 kB is 1,000 bytes
  - mega: 1 MB is 1,000 kilobytes
  - giga: 1 GB is 1,000 megabytes
  - tera: 1 TB is 1,000 gigabytes.
- Historically the terms kilobyte, megabyte, etc. have often been used to represent powers of 2.
- The SI units of kilo, mega and so forth refer to values based on powers of 10. When referring to powers of 2 the terms kibi, mebi and so forth would normally be used.
- It is easy to get confused about the difference between kb, Kb, Mb, MiB, MB, TB, GB, bytes/s, bits/s.
- There is significant difference between data **size** and data **speed**; they are measured differently too.
- The difference not only lies in the 'b' (bit) and 'B' (byte), but also lies in the 'k' and 'K' or the 'm' or 'M' and so forth. Upper-case K/M is used in the storage industry and lower-case k/m is used in the telecommunication industry.
- In networking, speed is measured in bps ('b' is in lower case).
- Always use the lower-case 'b' in the case of networking and data speed handling:
  - Bits per second or bits/sec or bits/s are the other names of bps.
  - Bytes per second or bytes/sec or bytes/s are the other names of Bps.

> A single binary digit (0 or 1) is called a **bit**. For example, 11010 is five bits long. The word bit is made up from the words 'binary digit'.
>
> A **byte** is a group of eight binary digits ('0' or '1').

Data compression

- **Data compression** is a set of steps for packing data into a smaller 'electronic space' (fewer data bits), while still allowing for the original data to be accessed and used.
- This is often achieved by eliminating the repetition of identical sets of data bits (redundancy).
- Compression results in much smaller storage space requirements and is often much faster for communications. Compressed data works more effectively on our mobile phones and portable computers.

> **Data compression** is a reduction in file size to reduce download times and storage requirements.

Run-length encoding

- Run-length encoding (RLE) is a data compression algorithm supported by most bitmap file formats, for example TIFF, BMP and PCX.
- RLE is suited for compressing any type of data, but the content of the data affects the compression ratio achieved by RLE.
- RLE works by reducing the size of a repeating string.
- A repeating string is called a run, and is typically encoded into two bytes:
  ○ The first byte represents the number of characters in the run and is called the run count.
  ○ The second byte is the value of the character in the run, which is in the range of 0 to 255, and is called the run value.

Compression with text

- For an easy-to-understand example of compression with text, we will look at the following text: 'run–length encoding makes files smaller; smaller files use run–length encoding'.
- If each character and space in this sentence takes up one unit of memory, the whole thing would have a file size of 78 bytes.
- There are patterns in our sentence. Most words in the sentence appear twice. Only 'makes' and 'use' appear just once.
- But to make use of this pattern we would need to create a dictionary, which is simply a way of cataloguing pieces of data, in this case words.
- If we created a dictionary using a numbered index to represent each word, it could look something like this:
  1 run
  2 length
  3 encoding
  4 makes
  5 files
  6 smaller
  7 use
- We could now write the text using our numbered index as: 1 2 3 4 5 6; 6 5 7 1 2 3.
- The compressed file would use less memory.
- In practice, it will be a little larger as we will need to store our index alongside the data or it will be impossible to read the file, but the example gives you a good understanding of how this system could work.

Lossless compression

- In lossless compression, all the original data can be recovered when the file is uncompressed.
- With lossless compression, every bit of data that was originally in the file remains, so nothing is lost when the file is uncompressed.
- The name for this type of algorithm is lossless = we lose nothing.

Lossy compression

- If you take a photograph of a country view, large parts of the picture may look the same – the whole sky is blue and the grass is green, for example – but most of the individual pixels are a little bit different.
- The lossless system will not compress the file very well; it could even make the file larger.
- To make this picture smaller without compromising the resolution, you would have to change the colour value for certain pixels to make them the same before compression.
- If the picture had a lot of blue sky, the algorithm could pick one colour of blue that could be used for every pixel and replace all the variations with the same colour.
- Whilst you will lose the exact information for these different shades of blue and it will never be recoverable (hence 'lossy' compression), for most uses the difference will not be noticeable.

Huffman encoding

- We can also use a binary tree to reduce the storage size of text.
- To encode English text, we would need 26 lower-case letters, 26 upper-case letters and some punctuation. Let's say that we could get by with 64 characters.
- We could achieve this with six bits but as ASCII uses seven we will also allow up to seven bits for each character. In text, some characters are more frequent than others.
- We need a system where different characters can be different bit widths, but we also need to tell the system where each character begins and ends without using additional bits for this.
- As an example, consider the word ABRACADABRA:

Letter	Frequency
A	5
R	2
B	2
C	1
D	1

- We now assign a binary value to each letter.
- Each assignment must be **unique** and easily distinguished from the other assignments.
- D and C are the least frequent letters used in our word so we will give them the largest assignment of four bits.
- As the letter A is the most frequently used in our word, we will give it the shortest assignment of one bit.

- R and B are the next most frequent so we will give R a two-bit assignment and B an assignment of three bits, as shown in the table:

Letter	Assignment
A	0
R	11
B	100
C	1010
D	1011

- Using these assignments we can write ABRACADABRA using our assignments as:

'A'0, 'B'100, 'R'11, 'A'0, 'C'1010, 'A'0, 'D'1011, 'A'0, 'B'100, 'R'11, 'A'0, which is 01001101010010110100110.

- We can find the letters as they have unique assignments. We can find each individual letter easily. This word would now only need 23 bits.
- We can then calculate the bits saved: 77 − 23 = 54.
- Let's look at a simple Huffman binary tree and how we can use it to read the code.
- Looking at the tree, we can work out the word from the code: in 01001101010010110100110, the first 0 can only be an A, a 100 can only be a B, 11 a letter R, etc.
- To see how we build the tree in the first place we will look at how it is constructed. In Huffman coding, we assign bits by creating a binary tree where the children are the encoding units with the smallest frequencies.
- As you are unlikely to use Huffman coding for a single word, we will examine a sentence with our word inside it.
- In practice, we would have many more characters used but, as an example of how the system works, we will stay with our five letters and find the assignments for these letters only.
- The letter frequencies for our sentence are as follows:

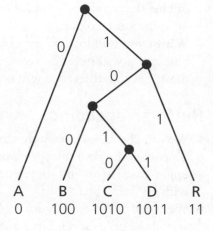

Letter	Frequency
A	40
B	20
R	20
C	10
D	10

- The smallest number of occurrences in our sentence are of C and D, so in Huffman coding we must connect these using a binary tree. This creates a new node above C and D which would be called C+D as it is a connection of these two child nodes.
- In a binary tree there can only be two nodes. C+D now has a frequency value of 20 as there are 10 Cs and 10 Ds and the parent node value will be the two child frequencies added together.

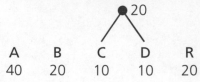

- We continue adding our letters until the tree is complete.

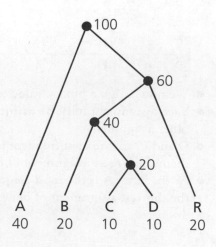

● Finally, we assign 0 to all the left branches and 1 to all the right branches.

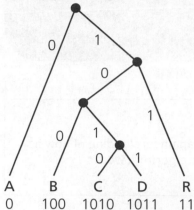

A B   C   D   R
0 100 1010 1011 11

● Each encoding now shows us a path from the root and each path terminates at a leaf. The path to R is 11, to B is 100. Our assigned values for all the letters are as shown in the table:

Letter	Assignment
A	0
B	100
C	1010
D	1011
R	11

● Each is unique, so no bit string is a prefix of any other bit string. We have just created an example of Huffman encoding.

Exam practice

1 One nibble is equal to: [1]
  a) 1 bit   **b)** 2 bits   **c)** 4 bits   **d)** 8 bits

2 What does the term 'word length' refer to? [2]

3 Which statement is valid? [1]
  a) 1 KB = 1024 bytes   **c)** 1 MB = 1000 kilobytes
  b) 1 MB = 2048 bytes   **d)** 1 KB = 1000 bytes

4 Bit stands for: [1]
  a) binary digit   **c)** a part of byte
  b) bits of a system   **d)** all of these

5 A byte consists of: [1]
  a) 1 bit   **b)** 4 bits   **c)** 8 bits   **d)** 16 bits

6 One kilobyte refers to: [1]
  a) 1000 bytes   **b)** 1024 bytes   **c)** 8000 bytes   **d)** 8192 bytes

7 The term 'gigabyte' refers to: [1]
  a) 1000 bytes   **c)** 1000 megabytes
  b) 1000 kilobytes   **d)** 1000 gigabytes

8 Which one is the largest? [1]
  a) kilobyte   **b)** petabyte   **c)** terabyte   **d)** gigabyte

9 Explain how compression is achieved with text. In this question you will be marked on your ability to use good English, to organise information clearly and to use specialist vocabulary where appropriate. [6]

10 Explain what is meant by the term 'run-length encoding'. [6]

11 Describe what is meant by the term 'data compression'. [6]

12 Describe the steps required to build an algorithm for a Huffman tree. [3]

Answers on p. 119

ANSWERS CHECKED

3.4 Encryption

Specification references

You must be able to:

3.4.1 demonstrate an understanding of the need for data encryption

3.4.2 demonstrate an understanding of how a Caesar cipher algorithm works

Cryptographic algorithms

REVISED

- If you program anything that works over the internet and needs to handle confidential information, you will have to use what are called 'cryptographic' algorithms to keep the system secure.
- Cryptographic algorithms are sequences of rules that are used to encrypt and decrypt code. They are algorithms that protect data by making sure that unwanted people can't access it.
- Most security algorithms involve the use of encryption, which allows two parties to communicate but uses coded messages so that third parties, such as hackers, cannot understand the communications.
- Encryption algorithms are used to transform plain text into something that cannot be understood. The encrypted data is then decrypted to restore it, making it understandable to the intended party.

Caesar cipher

REVISED

- The **Caesar cipher** is one of the oldest types of cipher. It is named after Julius Caesar, who is said to have used it to send messages to his generals over 2,000 years ago.
- In a Caesar cipher there is one shared key. With a Caesar cipher, an algorithm replaces each letter in a message with a letter further along in the alphabet using a number key.
- The cipher simply shifts the alphabet and is therefore also called a shift cipher.
- You need to know what the number key is to decipher the message. The number key is simply the number of letters you shift. The diagram shows a shift of three.

> **Caesar ciphers** are symmetric. There is one shared key. In a Caesar cipher, an algorithm replaces each letter in a message with a letter further along in the alphabet using a number key.

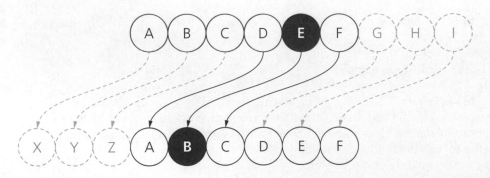

- Mathematically you would do this by numbering the letters of the alphabet from 0 to 25, as follows:

A B C D E F G H I J K L M N O P Q R S T U V W X Y Z

0   1   2   3   4   5   6   7   8   9   10 11 12 13 14 15 16 17 18 19 20 21 22 23 24 25

- Transforming the letters of the plain text into numbers, COMPUTER becomes 2 14 12 15 20 19 4 17.
- Then do the shift for every letter:
  - $2 + 3 \bmod 26 = 5$ (F)
  - $14 + 3 \bmod 26 = 17$ (R)
  - $12 + 3 \bmod 26 = 15$ (P)
  - $15 + 3 \bmod 26 = 18$ (S)
  - $20 + 3 \bmod 26 = 23$ (X)
  - $19 + 3 \bmod 26 = 22$ (W)
  - $4 + 3 \bmod 26 = 7$ (H)
  - $17 + 3 \bmod 26 = 20$ (U)
- The plain message COMPUTER becomes FRPSXWHU.

Exam practice

1 Create a Caesar cypher with a three-place shift to say 'Edexcel'.   [3]
2 What is a cryptographic algorithm?   [2]

Answers on p. 119

ANSWERS CHECKED ☐

3.5 Databases

Specification references

You must be able to:

3.5.1 demonstrate an understanding of the characteristics of structured and unstructured data

3.5.2 demonstrate an understanding that data can be decomposed, organised and managed in a structured database (tables, records, fields, relationships, keys)

- Databases use a series of tables to store data.
- A table simply refers to a two-dimensional representation of data stored in rows and columns. For example:

Steve	Cushing	steve@hodder.com
John	Wilson	john@hodder.com
Jess	Hadden	jess@hodder.com

- So we have a table with rows containing a person's details, and columns.
- Each table needs a unique name so that the database management system (often referred to as DBMS) can find the right one; we will call this table 'contacts'.
- Next, each column needs a name:

first_name	last_name	email_address
Steve	Cushing	steve@hodder.com
John	Wilson	john@hodder.com
Jess	Hadden	jess@hodder.com

Structured data

REVISED

- A database is a structured collection of similar information that you can search through. A database package is a program for storing information on a computer.
  - field: one piece of information.
  - record: a collection of fields about one person or subject.
  - file: a group of records on the same topic.

Key field

REVISED

- To make the database usable, we need to add a unique key to the table.
- Most database developers create their own column with a computer-generated unique number to act as the unique key, referred to as the database's key field.

first_name	last_name	email_address	key
Steve	Cushing	steve@hodder.com	1001
John	Wilson	john@hodder.com	1002
Jess	Hadden	jess@hodder.com	1003

Flat file databases

- We could just keep adding fields for any additional data.
- This would be called a flat file database, but these can be very slow, so most professional databases have different tables linked together.

Relational databases

- Rather than increasing the fields and getting a larger and more unmanageable flat file database, we could create another table.
- Let us say that each of the people in our table buys a product from an online shop. We could produce a new table of sales information.

number	product_name	product_code	item_id
10	Rise and Fall	B607	1001
2	Times Square	H766	1002
1	Home	L678	1003

- Now we need to link the two tables together, to relate the data in one table with another. This is where the relational database gets its name.
- As we have seen, a relational database is a group of data items assembled into a set of formatted tables in which data can be searched, accessed and interrogated in a multitude of different ways without having to reorganise the tables.
- The standard user interface to any relational database is the structured query language (SQL).
- By using SQL statements, interactive queries for information can be made to retrieve information from a relational database and used for gathering data for reports.

item_id	key
1001	1001
1002	1002
1003	1003

Key terms used in databases

Flat file database	A database with a single table.
Foreign key	A column or combination of columns that is used to establish and enforce a link between the data in two tables.
Form	A user interface used to input data into a database.
Primary key	A unique identifier.
Query	A query is used to search a database.
Record	Records are composed of fields, each of which contains one item of information.
Relational database	A database that is more than one table.
Report	Used to print out information from the database.
Table	A table is used to store records.

Exam practice

1 What is a database? [2]
2 For each of the headings below, state their purpose in a relational database. [8]
   a) Table   c) Row   e) Field   g) Primary key
   b) Record   d) Column   f) Query
3 Briefly describe the term 'index' when used in the context of a relational database. [6]

Answers on p. 119

ANSWERS CHECKED

4.1 Machines and computational modelling

Devices and computer systems

REVISED

- Peripheral (input/output) devices allow the computer to communicate with the outside world.

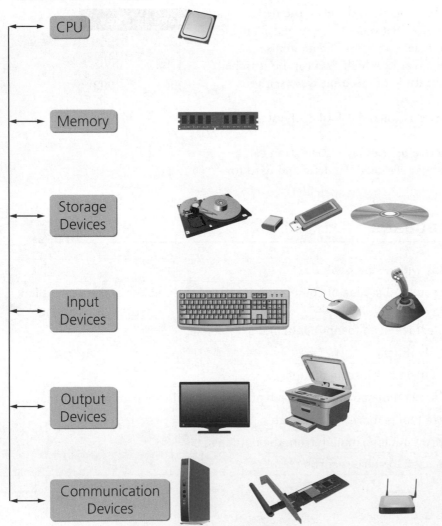

• The workings of the system follow the input–process–output model.

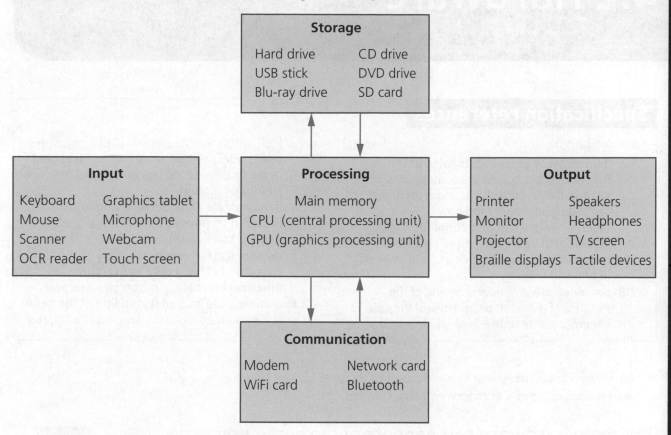

Computational modelling

REVISED

• Computational modelling is the use of mathematics, physics and computer science to study the behaviour of complex systems by computer simulation. A computational model contains numerous variables that characterise the system being studied.
• These models take a user input and via a set of predetermined rules they process the input and output useful predictions. They are as accurate as the data input to the system and the accuracy of the rules within the model.

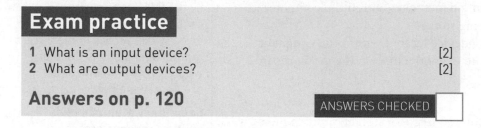

Exam practice

1 What is an input device?   [2]
2 What are output devices?   [2]

Answers on p. 120

ANSWERS CHECKED

4.2 Hardware

Specification references

You must be able to:

4.2.1 demonstrate an understanding of the function of the hardware components of a computer system (CPU, main memory, secondary storage), and how they work together with input and output devices

4.2.2 demonstrate an understanding of the function of different types of main memory (RAM, ROM, cache)

4.2.3 demonstrate an understanding of the concept of a stored program and the role of components of the CPU (control unit (CU), arithmetic/logic unit (ALU), registers, clock, address bus, data bus, control bus) in the fetch–decode–execute cycle (the Von Neumann model)

4.2.4 demonstrate an understanding of how data is stored on physical devices (magnetic, optical, solid state)

4.2.5 demonstrate an understanding of the concept of storing data in the 'cloud' and other contemporary secondary storage

4.2.6 demonstrate an understanding of the need for embedded systems and their functions

● Hardware is the name given to a collection of physical 'things' that, when put together in a certain way, form a system.

The main hardware components of the computer

REVISED ☐

Processor

● Carries out computation and has overall control of the computer.
● Also known as the central processing unit (CPU), it is situated on the computer motherboard.

Main memory

● Stores programs and data while the computer is running.
● Is fast access, directly accessible by the processor, limited in size and non-permanent.
● Computers can store data in **main memory** (within the computer itself) or **secondary memory** (backing storage).
● Main memory is any memory device located within the computer system itself, including separate memory chips on the motherboard.

Secondary memory

● Holds quantities of information too large for storage in main memory.
● Secondary memory is slower access than main memory, not accessible directly by the processor but can be used to keep a permanent copy of programs and data.

External system bus

● This allows communication of information between the component parts of the computer.

> **Main memory** (also called primary storage) is any form of memory that is directly accessible by the CPU, except for caches and registers. It is directly connected to the motherboard and is the place where programs and data are kept while being used.
>
> **Secondary memory** (also called secondary storage) is the place where software and data are kept when not in use.

Von Neumann architecture

- A Von Neumann-based computer:
  - uses one memory for both instructions and data
  - cannot distinguish between data and instructions in a memory location
  - executes programs by doing one instruction after the next in a serial manner using a fetch–decode–execute cycle.

Advantages of Von Neumann architecture

- The main advantage is that it simplifies the microcontroller chip design because only one memory is accessed.
- In microcontrollers, the most important thing is the contents of RAM (random access memory) and in the Von Neumann system it can be used for both variable (data) storage and program instruction storage.
- Another advantage is that it allows greater flexibility in developing software, particularly in the development of operating systems.

Disadvantages of Von Neumann architecture

- Whilst the advantages far outweigh the disadvantages, the problem is that there is only one bus (pathway) connecting the memory and the processor so only one instruction or data item can be fetched at a time. This means the processor may have to wait longer for the data/instruction to arrive. This is referred to as the Von Neumann bottleneck.
- The above reason can also lead to a system crash as there may be confusion between data and instructions.

The CPU (central processing unit)

- This internal device is often referred to as the computer's brain and it is the piece of hardware that is responsible for the 'compute' in computer.
- If you did not have the **CPU**, you would not have a computer.
- The CPU's purpose is to process data and it does this by performing functions such as searching and sorting data, and calculating and decision-making using the data.
- What this means is that for every task you carry out on a computer, the central processing unit deals with all of the data processing.
- The CPU continuously reads instructions stored in main memory and executes them as required:
  - fetch: the next instruction is fetched to the CPU from main memory
  - decode: the instruction is decoded to work out what it is
  - execute: the instruction is executed (carried out).
- This may include reading/writing from/to main memory.
- A processor contains the following components:
  - arithmetic and logic unit: performs arithmetic and logical operations on data
  - control unit: fetches, decodes and executes instructions
  - internal buses: to connect the components
  - internal clock: derived directly or indirectly from the system clock.

> The central processing unit (**CPU**) is the electronic circuitry within a computer that carries out the instructions of a computer program.

Speed

The CPU undertakes instructions it receives from programs in what is called a cycle. The CPU contains a number of cores which operate at a certain speed.

Computer and microprocessor designers are driven by the need to improve computer performance to meet the ever increasing demands of computer users.

- The speed of the CPU is measured in how many cycles it can perform in a second. The name given to one cycle per second is a hertz.
- Early microprocessors had clock speeds measured in kHz (thousands of cycles per second). A CPU that processes one million cycles per second is said to have a speed of one megahertz.
- A CPU that can handle one billion cycles per second is said to have a clock speed of one gigahertz. Obviously, clock speed is an important factor in determining performance.
- Most modern processors operate at speeds of over 1 GHz (one thousand million cycles per second).

Arithmetic and logic unit

- The **arithmetic logic unit** (called the ALU) is a major component of the central processing unit of a computer system.
- ALUs routinely perform the following:
  - logical operations: including AND, OR, NOT
  - logical comparisons
  - bit-shifting operations: shifting the positions of the bits by a certain number of places to the right or left, which is considered a multiplication operation
  - arithmetic operations: bit addition and subtraction.

> The **arithmetic logic unit** (ALU) performs all the arithmetic and logical operations within the CPU.

The control unit (CU)

- The **control unit** (CU) is inside the CPU and is used to control the flow of data within the system.
- CU functions are as follows:
  - controls sequential instruction execution
  - interprets instructions
  - guides data flow through different computer areas
  - regulates and controls processor timing
  - sends and receives control signals from other computer devices
  - handles tasks, such as fetching, decoding, execution handling and storing results.

> The **control unit** (CU) is inside the CPU and is used to control the flow of data within the system.

Internal buses

- An internal **bus** is a type of data bus that only operates inside the computer or system. It carries data and operations like a standard bus; however, it is only used for connecting and interacting with internal computer components.
- The CPU bus is internal to the CPU and is used to transport data to and from the ALU.
- A bus is a collection of wires through which data is transmitted from one component to another.
- Increasing the clock speed will increase the number of data fetches that can be made per second.
- Increasing the data bus width will increase the amount of data that can be fetched each time.

> A **bus** is part of the computer architecture that transfers data and signals between all the components of the computer. It is a collection of wires through which data is transmitted from one component to another.

Internal clock

- A clock is a signal used to synchronise things inside the computer.
- The beginning of each clock cycle is when the clock signal goes from 0 to 1.
- The clock signal is measured in hertz (Hz), which is the number of clock cycles per second. A clock of 100 MHz means that in one second there are 100 million clock cycles.

Factors affecting processor performance

- There are a number of things in the computer architecture that can affect the processor performance. The following are the most important factors.

Number of cores

- A CPU can contain one or more processing units.
- Each unit is called a core.
- Each core contains an ALU, control unit and registers.

Clock speed

- The clock speed of a processor is stated in megahertz (MHz) or gigahertz (GHz).
- Basically, the faster the clock, the more instructions the processor can complete per second.

On-board cache

- The on-board cache is a type of high-performance RAM built directly into the processor. Cache has both size and type.
- It enables the CPU to access repeatedly used data directly from its own on-board memory.

Cache memory

- Cache memory uses the faster but more expensive static RAM chips rather than the less expensive, but slower, dynamic RAM chips which are used for most of the main memory.
- Cache memory is connected to the processor by the 'backside' bus.
- Normally, whole blocks of data are transferred from main memory into cache, while single words are transferred along the backside bus from the cache to the processor.

L1 and L2 cache

- Most modern chips also have level 1 (L1) cache.
- This is similar to L2 cache, but the cache is actually on the same chip as the processor. This means that it is even faster to access than L2 cache.

Embedded systems

- An embedded system is a system that has computer hardware with software embedded in it as one of its components. As embedded systems are small, low cost and simple they have become very popular and are now indispensable in our lives. They are found everywhere, from kitchens to hospitals.
- Embedded systems frequently have more limited resources than PCs.
- Embedded systems usually focus on dedicated tasks, but PCs are general-purpose computers.
- Embedded systems usually require minimal human intervention.
- Embedded systems that are being used every day:
  - Aircraft (flight landing gear systems and many other systems from sensors to controllers)
  - All gym equipment from treadmills to cycling equipment
  - ATMs
  - Car systems (pressure monitoring systems, airbags, power windows and GPS systems)
  - Microwave ovens
  - Military applications
  - Mobile phones
  - Pacemakers
  - Robots
  - Toys
  - TV remotes (and all other remote control devices)
  - Vending machines
  - Washing machines (including dishwashers and drying machines)
  - and many more …

Actuators and sensors

- Microprocessors use actuators and sensors to function.

Actuators

- An actuator is used to move or control the output.
- It is a type of motor for moving or controlling a mechanism or system. To operate it needs a source of energy, usually in the form of an electric current, hydraulic fluid pressure or pneumatic pressure.
- The **actuator** converts that energy into motion.

Sensors

- A **sensor** is a converter that measures a physical quantity and converts it into a signal. The microcontroller uses this signal to make a decision.
- Microcontrollers need digital signals.

An **actuator** is used to move or control the output. It is a type of motor for moving or controlling a mechanism or system. To operate it needs a source of energy, usually in the form of an electric current, hydraulic fluid pressure or pneumatic pressure. The actuator converts that energy into motion.

A **sensor** is a device that can detect physical conditions such as temperature, weight, light, sound, etc.

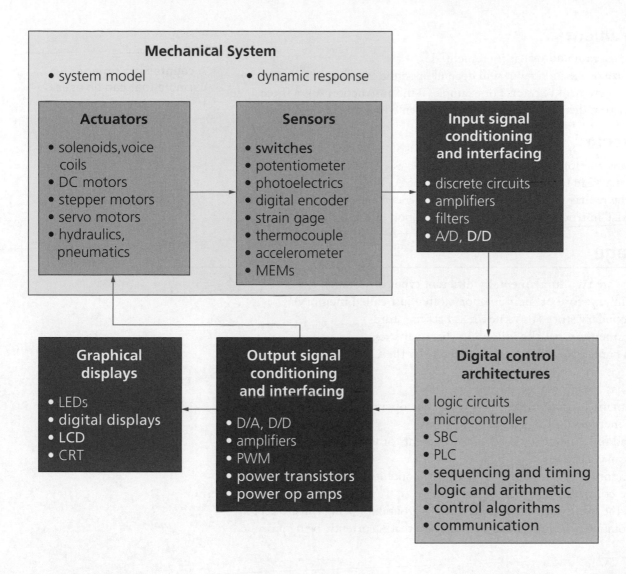

Fetch, decode and execute

- To **execute** a machine code program it must first be loaded, together with any data that it needs, into main memory (RAM).
- Once loaded, it is accessible to the CPU which fetches one instruction at a time, decodes it and executes it.
- Fetch, decode and execute are repeated until a program instruction to HALT is encountered. This is known as the fetch–decode–execute cycle.

> In computer science, to **execute** is the process of carrying out an instruction by a computer.

1 Fetch

- The instruction is fetched from the memory location whose address is contained in the program counter and placed in the instruction register.
- The instruction will consist of an operation code and possibly some operands. The operation code determines which operation is carried out. The term opcode is usually used as shorthand for operation code.

2 Decode

- The pattern of the opcode is interpreted by the control unit and the appropriate actions are taken by the electronic circuitry of the CU.
- These actions may include the fetching of operands for the instruction from memory or from the general-purpose registers.

3 Increment

- The program **counter** is incremented.
- The size of the increment will depend upon the length of the instruction in the increment register. For example, if this instruction was a three-byte instruction then the PC would be incremented by three.

4 Execute

- The instruction in the instruction register is executed.
- This may lead to operands being sent to the ALU for arithmetic processing and the return of the result to one of the general-purpose registers. When a HALT instruction is received then execution of this program ceases.

Storage

REVISED

- There are two fundamentally different types of storage:
  ○ primary store or main memory (often just called memory)
  ○ secondary store (also known as backing store).
- Main memory has the following characteristics:
  ○ Its contents can be accessed directly by the CPU.
  ○ It has very fast access times.
  ○ It has a relatively small capacity.
- The main/primary memory is where the operating system resides. This memory is divided into two types:
  ○ read only memory (ROM), the contents of which are retained (non-volatile)
  ○ random access memory (RAM), the contents of which are lost when the computer is turned off (volatile).
- With the Von Neumann architecture the program(s) being run are kept in the computer memory along with the data that is currently being processed.

ROM

- ROM is memory that cannot be changed by a program or user.
- ROM retains its memory even after the computer is turned off.
- ROM is used to store the instructions for the computer to boot up when it is turned on.
- ROM is also used to store software that needs to be available when the computer is turned on (such as the instructions for booting the computer) or software that will never change, such as the BIOS.

EEPROM

- EEPROM is electrically erasable programmable read-only memory.
- As such it is a user-modifiable read-only memory (ROM) and can be erased and reprogrammed without being removed from the computer, as is the case with other EPROM chips.
- But the chip does have to be erased and reprogrammed in its entirety, not selectively.

RAM

- RAM is a fast temporary type of memory in which programs, applications and data are held. RAM holds things while the computer is on and they are running:
  ○ the operating system
  ○ applications software.
- If a computer loses power, all data stored in its RAM is lost.

Cache memory

- Cache is simply very fast memory.
- Cache memory is a special type of RAM.
- The cache is almost always located on the same microchip as the CPU.
- Traditionally, cache is categorised in levels that describe its closeness and the accessibility of the cache to the microprocessor.
- Cache types:
  - Level 1 (L1) cache is extremely fast but relatively small and is usually embedded in the processor chip (CPU), which is why it is called level 1. It is closest to the processor. Level 1 cache usually ranges in size from 8 KB to 64 KB.
  - Level 2 (L2) cache is often larger than L1 but one stage further from the processor. It may be located on the CPU or on a separate chip.
  - Level 3 (L3) cache is typically specialised memory that works to improve the performance of L1 and L2. It can be significantly slower than L1 or L2, but is usually double the speed of RAM.

Accessing memory

- Memory can be accessed sequentially or randomly.
- To go from file A to file Z in a sequential access system, you must pass through all files in order.
- Sequential access is also called serial access.
- Direct or random access refers to the ability to access data at random.
- In a random access system, you can jump directly to file Z.
- Disks are examples of random access media.

Secondary storage

- Secondary storage is considered to be any non-volatile storage mechanism external to the CPU.
- Secondary storage is used to save permanent copies of your files.
- The majority of secondary storage devices are used for long-term storage.
- They are also used to:
  - backup data
  - add more storage space for files, pictures, videos, etc.
  - transfer files between computers
  - easily transport files
  - share files over a network.
- There are three main types of secondary storage:
  - Magnetic storage uses magnetic fields to store the data. Examples are hard disk drives or magnetic tapes.
  - Optical storage stores data by means of lasers 'burning' a disk. Examples are CD-ROM, DVD, Blu-ray.
  - Solid-state storage uses no moving parts at all, only memory chips. Examples are USB drives, SSD hard drives.

Magnetic storage devices (MSD)

REVISED

- A magnetic hard disk drive (HDD) uses moving read/write heads that contain electromagnets.
- These create a magnetic charge on the disk's surface, which contains iron particles that can be given a magnetic charge in one of two directions.

● Each magnetic particle's direction represents 0 (off) or 1 (on). These represent a bit of data that the CPU can recognise.

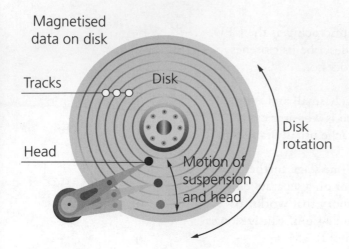

Magnetised data on disk

Tracks

Disk

Head

Disk rotation

Motion of suspension and head

Advantages of magnetic storage

● Very large data storage capacity.
● Stores and retrieves data much faster than an optical disk.
● Data is not lost when you switch off the computer, as it is with RAM.
● Cheap per MB compared with other storage media.
● Can easily be replaced and upgraded.

Disadvantages of magnetic storage

● Hard disks have moving parts, which can fail.
● Crashes can damage the surface of the disk, leading to loss of data.
● Easily damaged if dropped.
● Uses a large amount of power compared with other media.
● Can be noisy.

Exam tip

In extended writing questions, which are usually indicated by the command words 'compare' or 'contrast', explore both sides of an argument.

Optical storage devices (OSD)

REVISED

● An optical drive uses reflected light to read data.
● The optical disk's surface is covered with tiny dents (pits) and flat spots (lands), which cause light to be reflected off them differently.
● When an optical drive shines light into a pit, the light is not reflected back.
● This represents a bit value of 0 (off). When the light shines on a flat surface (land), it reflects light back to the sensor, representing a bit value of 1 (on).

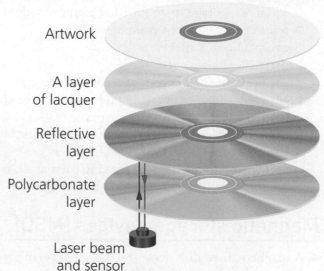

Artwork

A layer of lacquer

Reflective layer

Polycarbonate layer

Laser beam and sensor

Advantages of optical storage devices

● Easy to store and carry.
● Optical disks can be read by a number of devices such as audio and TV systems.
● Very easy to use.
● Long lasting if looked after properly.

Disadvantages of optical storage devices

- Data on write-once disks (CDR, DVDR and DRR) are permanent and cannot be changed.
- Optical disks require special drives to read/write.
- Optical storage is expensive per GB/TB in comparison with other methods.
- There are no standards for longevity tests.
- Can easily be scratched and damaged by heat and light.
- Easily broken.

Solid-state disks (SSD)

- Solid-state disks contain no moving parts.
- They are found in three common formats:
  - hard disk replacements
  - memory cards
  - USB flash drives.
- They record data using special transistors that retain their state even when there is no power to them.

Advantages of solid-state disks

- Read speeds are faster than for normal hard drives.
- Because there is no moving actuator arm like on a hard disk drive, they are faster in reading and, in some cases, writing data.
- They are also more rugged so are not as easily damaged when dropped.
- Solid-state hard drives have non-volatile memory, which means that data is stable.
- They are lightweight.
- They are very durable.
- They are free from mechanical problems.
- They require less power than magnetic drives.
- They are silent in use.

Disadvantages of solid-state disks

- They have limited storage capacity compared with normal magnetic hard drives.
- Random write speeds of solid-state drives can be four times slower than for normal magnetic hard drives.
- The cost per MB stored is higher than for magnetic drives.

Cloud storage

- Cloud storage means 'the storage of data online in the cloud'.
- In cloud storage, data is stored and is accessible from multiple distributed and connected resources that comprise a cloud via the internet.
- Given the many advantages, Apple, Google and Microsoft have all developed cloud-based data stores.

Advantages of cloud storage

- Unlimited storage capacity. Cloud computing offers limitless storage.
- Automatic backup. On a computer, a hard disk crash can destroy all your valuable data if it is stored on the device, but if it is in the cloud a computer crash shouldn't affect any of your data.
- Universal access. You don't carry your files and documents with you, they stay in the cloud, and you access them whenever you have a computer or mobile device and an internet connection. All your documents are instantly available wherever you are.
- Device independence. The user is not limited to working on a document stored on a single computer or network. You can change computer and even change to your mobile device, and the documents follow you through the cloud.

Disadvantages of cloud storage

- Cloud storage requires a reliable internet connection. Cloud computing is impossible if you can't connect to the internet.
- Cloud storage will not work as well with low-speed connections.
- Web-based apps and large documents and images require a lot of bandwidth.
- Loss of control. The user loses control over what happens to the data as this is managed by the cloud service provider.

Exam practice

1 The central processing unit is combination of: [1]
   a)   control and storage
   b)   control and output unit
   c)   arithmetic logic and input unit
   d)   arithmetic logic and control unit.
2 Describe cache memory and how it is used.   [6]
3 Which unit converts user data into machine readable form?   [1]
   a)   input unit   b)   output unit   c)   ALU   d)   control unit
4 EEPROM stands for: [1]
   a)   Electrically Erasable Programmable Read Only Memory
   b)   Electronic Erasable Programmable Read Only Memory
   c)   Easily Erasable Programmable Read Only Memory

5 Which unit is known as the nerve centre of the computer? [1]
  a) ALU   **b)** CU   **c)** memory   **d)** registers

6 What is access time? [1]
  a) seek time + latency time   **b)** seek time   **c)** latency time

7 Explain the different factors affecting the processing speed of the CPU. [8]

8 Explain the general structure of the CPU. [6]

9 Which part of the computer hardware is used for calculating and comparing? [1]
  a) disk unit   **b)** control unit   **c)** ALU   **d)** modem

10 Primary memory stores: [1]
  a) data alone   **b)** programs alone   **c)** results alone   **d)** all of these.

11 Which of the following is not a primary storage device? [1]
  a) magnetic tape   **b)** magnetic disk   **c)** optical disk   **d)** all of these

12 What does CD-ROM stand for? [1]
  a) Compactable Read Only Memory
  b) Compact Data Read Only Memory
  c) Compactable Disk Read Only Memory
  d) Compact Disk Read Only Memory

13 What does the disk drive of a computer do? [1]
  a) rotate the disk
  b) read the disk
  c) load a program from the disk into the memory
  d) both (b) and (c)

14 Primary memory stores: [1]
  a) data alone   **b)** programs alone   **c)** results alone   **d)** all of these.

15 What is the use of the registers in a CPU? [2]

16 What is a program counter? [2]

17 The instructions for starting the computer are housed on: [1]
  a) random access memory
  b) CD-ROM
  c) read-only memory chip
  d) all of the above

18 Secondary storage devices can store data but they cannot perform which of the following? [1]
  a) arithmetic operations
  b) logic operations
  c) fetch operations
  d) any of the above

19 Which device can understand the difference between data and programs? [1]
  a) input device   **b)** output device   **c)** memory   **d)** microprocessor

20 Which of the following is a read-only memory storage device? [1]
  a) memory stick   **b)** CD-ROM   **c)** hard disk   **d)** none of these

21 The central processing unit (CPU) consists of: [1]
  a) input, output and processing
  b) control unit, primary storage and secondary storage
  c) control unit, arithmetic logic unit and primary storage
  d) control unit, processing and primary storage.

22 Which unit converts computer data into human readable form? [1]
  a) input unit   **b)** output unit   **c)** ALU   **d)** control unit

23 The full form of ALU is: [1]
  a) Arithmetic Logic Unit
  b) Array Logic Unit
  c) Application Logic Unit
  d) None of the above.

24 What is a data bus? [1]

25 What is an address bus? [1]

26 Which of the following is a storage device? [1]
  a) tape   **b)** hard disk   **c)** CD-ROM   **d)** all of these

Answers on p. 120

ANSWERS CHECKED ☐

4.3 Logic

Specification references

You must be able to:

4.3.1 construct truth tables for a given logic statement (AND, OR, NOT)

4.3.2 produce logic statements for a given problem

Logic gates

REVISED ☐

- Logic gates can be understood better if you think of simple switches. Logic functions depend on **binary** bits of information.
- A simple switch is either open or closed.
- The bits could be represented by a yes or a no, or can be on (conducting) or off (not conducting).
- Whatever the two states might be, we will call one of the states a 1 and the other a 0. It doesn't matter which we call 1 and which we call 0 if we are consistent, but we will call the closed or conducting state of a switch 1 and the open or non-conducting state 0.

> **Binary** is a system of numbers using only two digits, 0 and 1 (also called the base 2 system), unlike the decimal (or denary) system in everyday use that uses 0 to 9 (base 10).

OR GATE

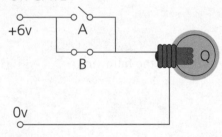

OR gates

REVISED ☐

- For a two-input OR gate, the output Q is true if **either** input A OR input B is true, giving the **Boolean** expression: Q = A or B.

$$\text{Two inputs} \Rightarrow \text{One output}$$

$$\frac{0}{0} \Rightarrow 0 \quad \frac{1}{0} \Rightarrow 1 \quad \frac{0}{1} \Rightarrow 1 \quad \frac{1}{1} \Rightarrow 1$$

> A **Boolean** expression is an expression that when evaluated is either true or false.
>
> A **truth table** is a diagram used to show the value of a Boolean expression for all possible variable combinations.

- We show this in the form of what is called a **truth table**. The truth table specifies the state of the system for each state of the switches:

Inputs		Outputs
A	B	Q
0	0	0
0	1	1
1	0	1
1	1	1

AND gates

- We could also look at how a series of switches makes an AND circuit. That is, all switches must be in the 1 state for the system to be in the 1 state (conducting).
- For a two-input AND gate, the output Q is true if **both** input A AND input B are true, giving the Boolean expression: Q = A and B.
- The truth table for the system would look like this:

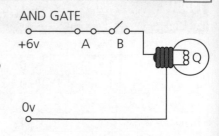

AND GATE

Inputs		Outputs
A	B	Q
0	0	0
0	1	0
1	0	0
1	1	1

- AND yields TRUE only if both values are TRUE:
  - FALSE and FALSE = FALSE
  - FALSE and TRUE = FALSE
  - TRUE and FALSE = FALSE
  - TRUE and TRUE = TRUE

NOT gates

- Unlike AND and OR gates, NOT gates have only one input and one output.
- The output is exactly the opposite of the input, so if the input is a 0, the output is a 1 and vice versa.
- NOT is a unary operator – it is applied to only one value and inverts it:
  - NOT TRUE = FALSE
  - NOT FALSE = TRUE
- The truth table would look like this:

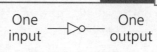

Inputs	Outputs
0	1
1	0

Constructing truth tables with more inputs

- We can easily create a circuit diagram from the description of the logic using these symbols.
- Let's say we want a system where we have four inputs, A, B, C and D. We want a circuit that outputs TRUE if either A AND B or C AND D are TRUE.

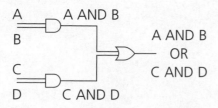

● Part of the truth table would look like this:

Inputs				Outputs
A	B	C	D	
1	1	1	0	1
1	1	0	1	1
0	1	0	1	0
1	0	1	0	0
1	1	1	1	1
1	0	1	1	1
0	1	1	1	1

Exam practice

1 Consider the following sentence:
When the door is open and it is cold outside I have to wear my coat.
Write this out as a Boolean expression. [2]

2 Write a piece of pseudo-code to use a REPEAT loop and Boolean expression that will print out all the even numbers from 2 to 100. [5]

3 What is a Boolean data type? [4]

4 If the tyre is flat then I will have to remove it and take it to the garage.
Complete the truth table below to represent each basic statement. [5]

The tyre is flat.	The wheel has been removed.	Take the wheel to the garage.
	1	
1	0	
0	1	
0		

5 Annotate the circuit diagram below to show the Boolean outputs. Part of the diagram has been completed for you. [2]

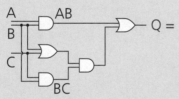

6 Complete the truth tables below: [8]
AND gate:

A	B	Q
0	0	
0	1	
1	0	
1	1	

INPUT   OUTPUT

OR gate:

A	B	Q
0	0	
0	1	
1	0	
1	1	

INPUT   OUTPUT

Answers on p. 121

ANSWERS CHECKED

4.4 Software

Types of software

REVISED

- There are two main types of software:
  - Application software: These are items of software that perform a particular task such as word processing or desktop publishing.
  - Systems software (operating systems): These types of software control the running of hardware and the running of other software.

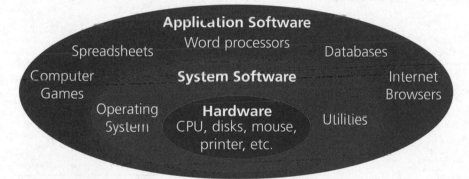

Operating systems

REVISED

An **operating system** is a piece of software that controls the operation of the systems hardware and the running of other software.

- Some examples of operating systems are:
  - Windows
  - Windows CE
  - Macintosh OS X (Mac OS X)
  - iOS (iPhoneOS)
  - Linux
  - Android
  - Blackberry (RIM OS)
  - Solaris (SunOS)
  - AIX
  - IOS (Cisco)
  - XOS (Extreme Networks)
  - IronWare OS (Foundry).

> An **operating system** is the software that controls all the hardware. It acts as an interface between the user and the hardware, and also between applications and the hardware.

- The operating system, as we can see, is actually not one but a collection of programs that control the system.
- The operating system is responsible for the management and control of all the computer's resources.
- This includes memory, processors, hard drives, monitoring I/O devices, etc.
- It not only handles the system resources, it also handles the application software that users run, security and file management.
- It also provides a link between the hardware and software.

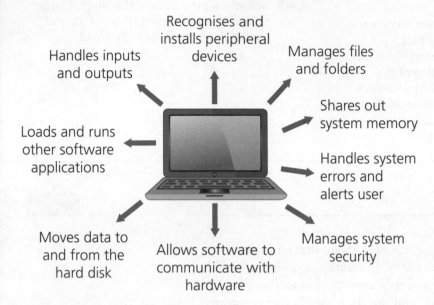

Recognises and installs peripheral devices

Handles inputs and outputs

Manages files and folders

Shares out system memory

Loads and runs other software applications

Handles system errors and alerts user

Moves data to and from the hard disk

Allows software to communicate with hardware

Manages system security

- All operating systems have certain common functions:
  - memory management
  - file management
  - security
  - provision of an interface
  - input and output
  - error reporting
  - utility software management.

Memory management

- Controls the system's **RAM**, controlling which locations in RAM programs are loaded into.
- The operating system handles the computer's memory and the sharing of the central processing unit (CPU). Its job is to make sure that each application gets the correct and adequate resources.
- It is also responsible for optimising the whole system.
- The operating system memory management functions include:
  - controlling the location of memory
  - dealing with the transfer of programs in and out of memory when the process no longer needs it or when the process has been ended
  - carrying out a process called scheduling where it manages the CPU, organising the use of memory between programs
  - organising processing time between programs and users
  - keeping track of processors and the status of any process running.

> **RAM** means random access memory. It is volatile, meaning that when power is interrupted, even for an instant, the contents are erased. RAM is not suitable for long-term storage of software and data.

File management

- Controls where and how files are saved to backing storage.
- The operating system handles the organisation and tracking of files and directories (folders). It also saves or retrieves these from a computer disk.
- The operating system does the following file management activities:
  - allows the user to perform tasks, including the creation of files and directories
  - allows the user to save files to a backing store
  - allows the user to rename, copy, move and delete files
  - keeps track of where files are located on the hard drive through either a file allocation table (FAT) or the New Technology File System (NTFS).

Security

- Computer systems often have multiple users.
- These users are often running multiple processes and these processes must be secure.
- The operating system maintains the security and access rights of users.
- The operating system does the following security activities:
  - controls the access of programs, processes and users to the computer resources
  - ensures that all access to system resources is controlled
  - ensures that external I/O devices are protected from invalid access attempts
  - provides authentication features for each user by means of a password.

Provision of an interface

- This is the means of interacting with the user.
- Most modern operating systems provide a GUI (graphical user interface).

Input and output

- Controls the sending and receiving of data to and from peripherals.
- The operating system does the following activities for device management:
  - acts as the I/O controller by keeping track of all I/O devices
  - decides which process gets the device, when and for how much time.

Error reporting

- The operating system provides useful feedback to users when errors occur.
- In any computer, the operating system deals with errors and user instructions.
- Errors can occur anytime and anywhere, including errors in the CPU, in I/O devices or in the memory hardware.
- The operating system does the following error management activities:
  - monitors the system for any errors that occur
  - takes appropriate actions to ensure correct operations
  - closes the system if errors are terminal.

Utility software management

- Other types of system software include utility software such as:

Software	Use
Virus scanner	To protect your system from trojans and viruses.
Disk defragmenter	To speed up your hard disk. Defragmentation picks up all those pieces of data that are spread across the drive and puts them back together again.
System monitor	To look at your current system resources.

Applications software

REVISED ☐

- **Application software** is programs that are designed to do a particular task.
- For example, a word processor and games are types of application program.
- Application software is computer software that causes a computer to perform useful tasks beyond the running of the computer itself.
- Such software is often called a software application, a program, application or an app.
- Examples of application software include:
  - ○ animation software
  - ○ audio editing
  - ○ data manipulation (databases and spreadsheets)
  - ○ digital audio editor
  - ○ graphic art software
  - ○ graphics editing
  - ○ image editing software
  - ○ image organisers
  - ○ media content creation/editing
  - ○ music sequencer
  - ○ presentation software
  - ○ text editors (word processors, desktop publishing)
  - ○ vector graphics editor
  - ○ video editing software
  - ○ web browser.

> **Application software**
> consists of programs that
> perform specific tasks,
> e.g. web browsers or word
> processing software.

Translation software

REVISED ☐

- The purpose of translator software is to convert program source code into machine code that can be executed on the processor.
- Translation software includes:
  - ○ assemblers
  - ○ compilers
  - ○ interpreters.
- Each performs a different task:

Assembler	An assembler (meaning one that assembles) is a computer program that translates assembly language to object code or machine language.
Compiler	A compiler translates the whole program (source code) into object code that can be stored and reused. A compiler makes faster, more secure code.
	A compiler also produces object code that is difficult to read, meaning competitors won't easily be able to steal or users hack the code.
Interpreter	Interpreters allow for code to run on multiple platforms. You can also debug and test code without having to recompile the entire source code.

Modelling software

- Real–world computer models tend to take one of two forms:
  - simulation models
  - optimisation models.
- For example, a model that helps a parcel delivery driver to take the shortest route to deliver a load of packages.

Simulation models

- Simulation models are used to clarify what would happen in a given situation.
- Simulation models are 'what if?' tools.
- Simulation models are used to model important aspects of the real world and show what could happen in certain scenarios.
- Flight simulators are one example of a simulation model. They help to expose pilots and designers to routine and unexpected flight circumstances.
- Computer games are also types of simulated modelling.

Exam practice

1 Discuss the role of the operating system. [8]
2 Explain the main memory management functions of the operating system. [6]
3 What is peripheral management? [6]
4 Which of the following is not a type of software? [1]
  - **a)** system software
  - **b)** application software
  - **c)** utility software
  - **d)** entertainment software
5 Programs designed to perform specific tasks are known as: [1]
  - **a)** system software
  - **b)** application software
  - **c)** utility programs
  - **d)** operating system
6 Operating systems, editors and debuggers come under? [1]
  - **a)** system software
  - **b)** application software
  - **c)** utilities
  - **d)** none of the above
7 A computer program that converts an entire program into machine language is called a: [1]
  - **a)** commander
  - **b)** simulator
  - **c)** compiler
  - **d)** interpreter
8 What do you call the programs that are used to find out possible faults and their causes? [1]
  - **a)** operating system extensions
  - **b)** cookies
  - **c)** diagnostic software
  - **d)** boot diskettes
9 Which programming languages are classified as low-level languages? [1]
  - **a)** Basic, COBOL, FORTRAN
  - **b)** Prolog 2, expert systems
  - **c)** knowledge-based systems
  - **d)** assembly languages
10 Which of the following provide machine-independent programs? [1]
  - **a)** high-level language
  - **b)** low-level language
  - **c)** assembly language
  - **d)** machine language

Answers on p. 121

4.5 Programming languages

Specification references

You must be able to:

4.5.1 demonstrate an understanding of what is meant by high-level and low-level programming languages, and an understanding of their suitability for particular tasks

4.5.2 demonstrate an understanding of what is meant by a compiler, an interpreter and an assembler, and know the advantages and disadvantages of each when translating programming languages

Computer languages

REVISED

- Computer languages are classified as:
  - high-level languages
  - low-level languages
  - assembly language
  - machine language (also referred to as machine code).
- High-level languages are much closer to human language.
- But a high-level language must use an interpreter, compiler or translator to convert a human-understandable program into a computer-readable language called machine code.
- Advantages of low-level languages:
  - If a programmer writes code in a low-level language, it does not require translation.
  - A low-level language does not need a compiler or interpreter to run; the processor for which the language was written is able to run the code without using these to translate the code into something it understands.
- Advantages of high-level languages over low-level languages:
  - Debugging is easier in a high-level language.
  - High-level programming techniques are applicable everywhere, even where computational resources are limited.
  - High-level languages make complex programming simpler.
  - Humans create fewer errors in high-level languages.
  - The length of the program is small compared with low-level languages.
  - The main advantage of high-level languages over low-level languages is that they are easier for humans to read, write and maintain.
  - Unlike low-level languages, the programmer does not need detailed knowledge of a particular internal computer architecture.

Assembly language

- **Assembly language** is a good example of a low-level language.
- Assembly language is at the level of telling the processor what to do.
- It is between machine language and high-level language.
- The word 'low' refers to the small or non-existent amount of abstraction between the language used and machine code.

> **Assembly language** is a low-level programming language. It uses mnemonic codes and labels to represent machine-level code. Each instruction corresponds to just one machine operation.

- A low-level language does not need a compiler or interpreter to run the program.
- Assembly languages have the same structure and set of commands as machine languages, but they enable a programmer to use names instead of numbers.
- Assembly language uses mnemonic codes for instructions and allows the programmer to introduce names for blocks of memory that hold data.
- Assembly language is designed to be easily translated into machine language.
- Like machine language, assembly language requires detailed knowledge of a particular internal computer architecture.

Machine code/language

- **Machine code** or machine language is a system of instructions and data executed directly by a computer's CPU.
- It is the lowest-level programming language.
- It is a set of instructions in binary that is used to represent operations and data in a machine.
- It is a collection of binary digits, or bits, that the computer reads and interprets.
- It is directly executable by a computer without the need for translation by a compiler or an assembler.
- It is the native language of the computer.

> **Machine code** is a set of instructions that a computer can execute directly. Machine code is written in a binary code, and each statement corresponds to one machine action. A computer's CPU can only understand instructions that are written in machine code.

Conversion of high-level language to low-level language

REVISED

- **Translators** are just computer programs which accept a program written in high-level or low-level language and produce an equivalent machine-level program as output.
- A translator is a computer program that translates one programming language instruction into another programming language instruction.
- High-level source code is translated into a low-level programming language; native code compilers change it into machine language for execution.
- Translators are of one of three types:
  - assembler
  - compiler
  - interpreter.

> A **translator** is a program to convert high-level or assembly-level commands into machine code.

Assembler

- An **assembler** converts assembly language source code into machine language.
- It is a program that takes high-level language and converts it into a pattern of bits (0s and 1s) that the computer runs to produce results.

> An **assembler** is a program that translates assembly language programs into machine code. Assembler directives are instructions to the translating programs.

Compiler

- A **compiler** is a program that compiles source code into executable instructions that a computer can understand.
- It compiles code and produces it in a new format before it runs.

> A **compiler** is a computer program that translates C, C++, BASIC, Pascal and similar high-level programming languages into machine language.

Interpreter

- An **interpreter** is a program that executes programming code directly.
- Interpreters can convert source code on a step-by-step, line-by-line and unit-by-unit basis into machine code.
- Interpreted languages are therefore read and executed directly, with no compilation stage.

> An **interpreter** is a program that executes a source program by reading it one line at a time and doing the specified operations immediately.

Interpreter	Compiler
Converts the program into machine code one statement at a time or calls a routine in its own code to execute the command.	Converts all the code of the program into machine code at the same time.
Takes less time to analyse the source code, but the overall program execution time is slower.	The first time the program is run it takes a large amount of time to analyse the source code, but once the compilation has taken place there is no need for any translation on subsequent runs of the program.
A client buying the software would need the translator software.	A client buying the software would not need the translator software.
Continues translating the program until the first error is met, in which case it stops.	Generates error messages after searching for all the errors in a program and then lists them.

Exam practice

1 Which of the statements below is valid about an interpreter? [1]
  a) It translates one instruction at a time.
  b) Object code is saved for future use.
  c) Repeated interpretation is not necessary.
  d) All of the above.

2 The translator program used for assembly language is called: [1]
  a) compiler
  b) interpreter
  c) assembler
  d) translator.

3 A computer program that converts an entire program into machine language is called a: [1]
  a) commander
  b) simulator
  c) compiler
  d) interpreter.

4 What is a compiler? [1]
  a) A compiler does a conversion line by line as the program is run.
  b) A compiler converts the whole of a higher-level program code into machine code in one step.
  c) A compiler is a general-purpose language providing very efficient execution.
  d) None of the above.

5 A compiler translates a program written in a high-level language into: [1]
  a) machine language
  b) an algorithm
  c) a debugged program
  d) none of these.

Answers on p. 121

ANSWERS CHECKED

5.1 Networks

Specification references

You must be able to:

5.1.1 demonstrate an understanding of why computers are connected in a network

5.1.2 demonstrate an understanding of the different types of networks (LAN, WAN) and usage models (client–server, peer-to-peer)

5.1.3 demonstrate an understanding of wired and wireless connectivity

5.1.4 demonstrate an understanding that network data speeds are measured in bits per second (Mbps, Gbps)

5.1.5 demonstrate an understanding of the role of and need for network protocols (Ethernet, Wi-Fi, TCP/IP, HTTP, HTTPS, FTP, POP3, SMTP, IMAP)

5.1.6 demonstrate an understanding that data can be transmitted in packets using layered protocol stacks (TCP/IP)

5.1.7 demonstrate an understanding of the characteristics of network topologies (bus, ring, star, mesh)

What is a network?

REVISED

- A computer network can be described as two or more computers connected together to share resources.
- The purpose of connecting computers together in a network is to exchange information and data.
- Networked computers can use resources of other computers.
- A computer network is a linked set of computer systems capable of sharing computer power and resources such as printers, large disk drives, CD-ROM and databases.
- Networks can be wired or wireless.
- There are two types of network:
  ○ local area network (LAN)
  ○ wide area network (WAN).

> **Exam tip**
>
> If your brain freezes during an exam, just start writing anything and you will soon start remembering more details.

Local area networks (LAN)

REVISED

- LANs are characterised by high-speed transmission over a restricted geographical area.
- If the LAN is too large, signals need to be boosted.
- A local area network is a computer network across one building or site, often owned and controlled/managed by a single person or organisation.

Wide area networks (WAN)

REVISED

- While LANs operate where distances are relatively small, wide area networks are used to link LANs that are separated by large distances that range from a few tens of metres to thousands of kilometres.
- The internet is the biggest example of a WAN.
- A WAN usually covers a wide geographic area, and is often under collective or distributed ownership.

Advantages and disadvantages of computer networks

REVISED

- There are a number of advantages to using networks; these include:
  - A network allows users to share software stored in a main system.
  - Files can easily be shared between users over a network.
  - Network users can communicate via email, instant messenger and VoIP.
  - Within networks, it is much more straightforward to backup data as it is all stored on the file server.
  - Networks allow data to be transmitted to remote areas that are connected within local areas.
  - Networking computers allows users to share common peripheral resources such as printers and fax machines, thereby saving money.
- There are also a number of disadvantages to using networks, which include:
  - Purchasing equipment such as cabling to construct a network and file servers can be costly.
  - The management of a large network is complicated, requiring training, and a specialist network manager usually needs to be employed.
  - In the event of a file server breaking down, the files contained on the server become inaccessible, although email might still work if it is stored on a separate email server. The computers can still be used but are isolated.
  - If a virus gets into the system through a network, it can easily spread to other computers.
  - There is a risk of hacking, particularly with wide area networks. Stringent security measures are required to prevent such abuse, such as a firewall.

Peer-to-peer networks

REVISED

- This describes a very simple network structure where shared resources such as printers are available but where there are very few other facilities.
- All computers on the network have similar specification and status.

Client–server networks

REVISED

- This method of network organisation requires one or more servers from which a number of clients may obtain services.
- The servers act as central resource managers for the network.
- A star topology is often used for this form of network.

Network hardware

REVISED

- Any electronic communications process requires the following components:
  - a source of the information
  - a transmitter to convert the information into data signals compatible with the communications channel
  - a communications channel
  - a receiver to convert the data signals back into a form the destination can understand
  - the destination of the information.
- The transmitter encodes the information into a suitable form to be transmitted over the communications channel.

- The communications channel moves this signal as electromagnetic energy from the source to one or more destination receivers.
- The channel may convert this energy from one form to another. This could be electrical or optical signals. It must maintain the integrity of the information so the recipient can understand the message sent by the transmitter.
- Network hardware will include:
  - stations
  - servers
  - file, print, web
  - passive components such as cables, connections, etc.
  - active components such as repeaters, hubs, switches.

Network interface card (NIC)

- Used to connect a computer to a network.
- Two different types:
  - wired
  - wireless.

Transmission medium

- The transmission medium is the material used to carry data over the network.
- There are two main forms:
  - wired, using cables
  - wireless (Wi-Fi).

Wired networks

- The two types of cables most commonly used are:
  - unshielded twisted pair (UTP)
  - optical fibre.
- Unshielded twisted pair is copper wire and is:
  - prone to interference – data carried using electrical signals
  - vulnerable to tapping
  - fairly cheap to install.

Optical fibre is made up of fine strands of glass; the data is carried using beams of light.
  - Although more expensive, it does not corrode.
  - Offers secure data transmission.
  - Has a much higher bandwidth over a much longer distance.

Coaxial	Twisted pair	Fibre optic
Electrical signal communication via the wires	Electrical signal communication via inner conductor of the wires	Optical signal communication via the glass fibres
High noise contamination	Medium noise contamination	Very low noise contamination
Can be affected by external magnetic interference	Less affected by external magnetic interference	Not affected by magnetic interference
Low bandwidth	Medium bandwidth	High bandwidth
Lowest cost of the three communication media	Moderately expensive compared to coaxial cable	Most expensive of the three communication media

Wireless networks

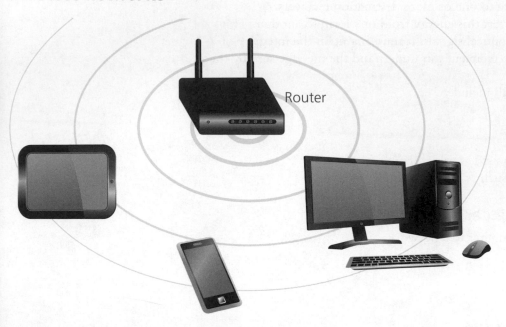

Router

- Possible methods of data transmission are:
  - Bluetooth
  - Wi-Fi.
- Bluetooth communication has the following properties:
  - Temporary short-range links between devices such as mobile phones, headsets, laptops.
  - Has a maximum range of 10 metres.
  - Transfer rate of between 1 and 3 Mbps.
- Wi-Fi is used in laptop computers, wireless routers, mobile phones and game consoles.
- Home Wi-Fi should be protected with a hard-to-guess password to prevent other people from using your broadband.
- If your broadband is stolen, the thief may be liable for prosecution; however, if they use it to do something illegal, you may be held responsible.
- Advantages and benefits of wireless networks:
  - The primary benefit of a wireless network is the freedom from cables.
  - It is also very convenient. The wireless nature of Wi-Fi networks allows users to access network resources from almost any convenient location.
  - With the growth of public wireless networks, users can also access the internet outside their normal work or home environment.
  - The initial setup of an infrastructure-based wireless network is relatively low cost as it requires no expensive cabling and a small network needs just a single access point.
  - Wireless networks are also easily expanded.

- Risks and disadvantages of wireless networks:
  - Whenever data is sent wirelessly, there is a chance that it can be intercepted.
  - The security used to encrypt the information determines how easy or hard it is to intercept the data.
  - Wi-Fi range, whilst sufficient for a typical home, can be insufficient in a larger building.
  - The speed of most wireless networks is much slower than the slowest common wired networks. In some situations where speed is essential a user may need a wired network.

Bandwidth

- Bandwidth is the amount of data that can be carried over a network at any one time.
- Data transfer speed means the same as bandwidth.
- Bandwidth is measured in:
  - Mbps – megabits per second
  - Gbps – gigabits per second.

Network stations

- The network station (often called the client) will normally comprise:
  - a PC
  - a network interface card (NIC), which allows the computer to communicate with the network
  - network operating systems.

Servers

- A network server is a computer which acts as a central storage point for files and applications.
- Servers also act as a connection point to shared peripherals such as printers.

Repeaters

- Due to loss of signal strength it is often necessary to use a repeater to boost the signal.
- A repeater is a hardware device to link together two cable segments.
- The repeater amplifies the signal it receives before passing it on.

Hubs

- A hub is a device that allows the interconnection of a group of users.
- A hub will forward any packet of data it receives over one port from one station to all of the remaining ports.
- Hubs are used in the star topology.

Switches

- A switch is 'smarter' than a hub and offers more bandwidth.
- A switch forwards data packets only to the appropriate port for the intended recipient.
- The switch establishes a temporary connection between the source and the destination.

Routers

- A router receives packets of data transmitted over a network; using the IP address, it forwards them to the correct destinations over the most efficient available path.

Network topology

- The network topology is the theoretical arrangement of components on a network.
- There are several network topologies that you need to be aware of:
  - ○ bus
  - ○ star
  - ○ mesh
  - ○ ring.

Bus topology

- Each device is connected to a main communication line called a **bus**.
- A single cable that functions as the backbone of the network acts as a shared communication medium that devices connect to via an interface connector.
- When a device wishes to communicate with another network device, it transmits a broadcast message onto the backbone wire that all the devices share.

> A **bus** is a collection of wires through which data is transmitted from one component to another.

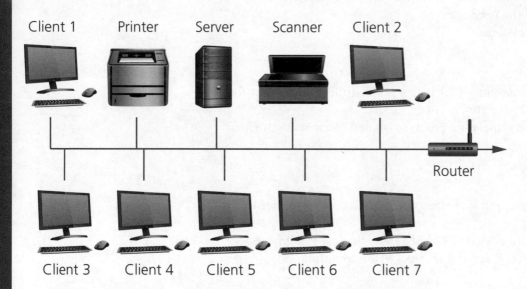

- The advantages of a bus topology are:
  - ○ It is easier and cheaper than other types of wired network to install as a consequence of requiring only a small quantity of cable.
  - ○ The lack of dependency on a central device as in a star topology makes the system more flexible.
- The disadvantages of a bus topology are:
  - ○ It performs well only for a limited number of computers because as more devices are connected, the performance of the network becomes slower as a consequence of data collisions.
  - ○ The impact of a single cable failure makes this type of wired network more vulnerable than other wired networks.

Star topology

- In the star topology all stations are connected to a central node, called a hub.
- Nearly all wired home networks use the star topology.
- This topology is, therefore, better understood than many other networks.

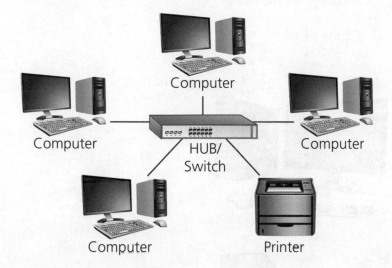

- The star network has a central connection point referred to as a 'hub node' that could be a device such as network hub, **switch** or router.
- The router on its own cannot be the hub node of a network. It needs to be linked to a switch, although in practice they are usually in the same box.
- The advantages of a star topology are:
  - Compared with the bus topology, star topology is better in terms of performance as signals don't necessarily get transmitted to all the workstations, although performance does depend on the capacity of the central hub.
  - The transmission medium is not shared so there can be multiple simultaneous communications.
  - Failure of one node or link doesn't affect the rest of network and it is easy to detect a failure and troubleshoot it as it allows isolation of each device within the network.
- The disadvantages of a star topology are:
  - The network operation ultimately relies on the correct functioning of the central hub, so if the central hub crashes it will lead to the failure of the whole network.
  - The use of a hub, router or switch as the central device and the additional cabling costs increase the overall cost of the network.
  - Performance and the number of nodes that can be added depend on the capacity of the central device.

A **switch** is the name given to a device for connecting multiple network devices.

Ring topology

- When every device has exactly two neighbours for communication purposes, the network layout is referred to as a ring topology.
- In a ring topology, all messages pass around in the same direction.
- This can be either clockwise or anticlockwise.
- As with the bus topology, should a failure in any cable occur or, in this case, if a device breaks down in the loop, it can take down the entire network.
- Ring topologies are found in some office buildings or school campuses.

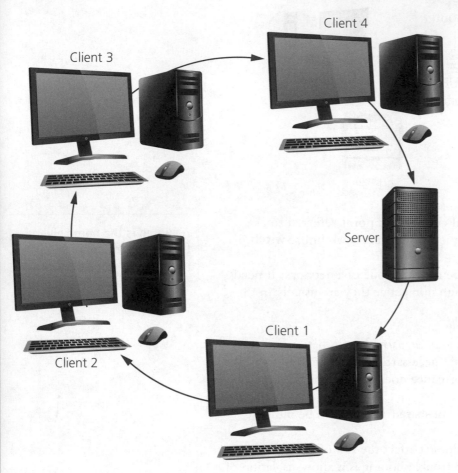

- An advantage of ring topology is that messages being sent between two workstations pass through all the intermediate devices, so a central server is not required for the management of this topology.
- The disadvantages of the ring topology are:
  - The failure of any cable within the network can cause the entire network to crash.
  - Alterations, maintenance or changes being made to the network nodes can impact the performance of the whole network.
  - Each device/computer needs additional software to handle the passing of messages.

Mesh topology

- The latest network arrangement is mesh networking.
- In mesh networks, each node connects to at least two other nodes and can connect to every other network node.
- If this happens, the arrangement is referred to as being 'fully connected'.
- A mesh network is the most expensive type of network to install.

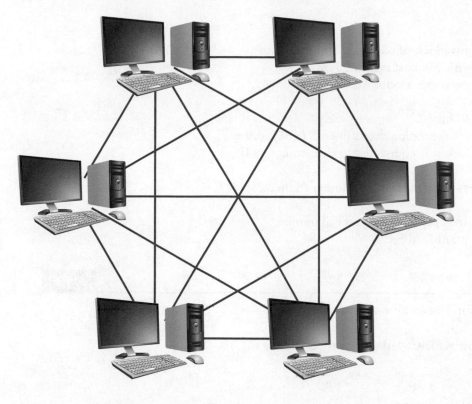

- The advantages of mesh networks are:
  - ○ Mesh networks can heal themselves automatically when a break occurs, so there's no interruption of service to any node.
  - ○ Mesh networks get bigger and faster as more nodes are added.
- The disadvantages of mesh networks are:
  - ○ This type of network involves more cabling or more wireless devices, leading to higher cost.
  - ○ Mesh networks are still in development and a full set of recognised standards has not yet been adopted.

Protocols

REVISED

- A **protocol** is a standard set of rules used to ensure the proper transfer of data between devices.
- In network design it is vital that a recognised protocol is used.
- You should be aware that the network layer is sometimes referred to as the internet layer and that the data link layer is sometimes referred to as the network interface layer.
- The importance of protocols is that they provide a standard way to interact among networked computers.

> A **protocol** is a set of rules or standards that controls communication between devices.

Addressing

REVISED

- Internet addressing is similar to the postal addressing system.
- The address system on the internet is called Internet Protocol (IP) addressing. In IPv4 an IP address assigned to a host is 32 bits long and is unique.
- An IP address has two parts:
  - ○ one part that is similar to the postal code
  - ○ the other part that is similar to the house address.
- They are known as the net id (netid) and the host id (hostid).

netid

- The netid identifies a contiguous block of addresses and is used to identify which particular network the host is located on.
- Another popular form of address is the Media Access Control (MAC) address.
- MAC addresses are six bytes (48 bits).
- The computer's own hardware configuration determines its MAC address.
- The configuration of the network it is connected to determines its IP address.
- The first half of a MAC address contains the ID number of the adapter manufacturer.
- The second half of a MAC address represents the serial number assigned to the adapter by the manufacturer.

TCP/IP

REVISED

- All networked computers communicate through what are called protocol suites.
- The most widely used and most widely available protocol suite is the TCP/IP protocol suite.
- TCP/IP is a four-layer system.

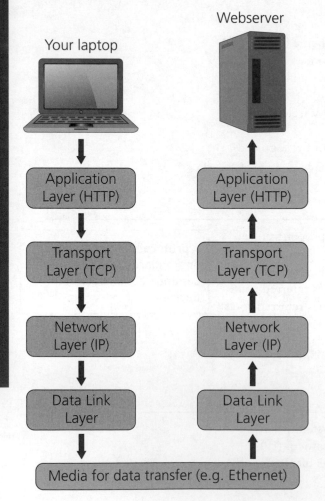

The application layer

- The application layer provides applications for file transfer, remote control and internet activities.
- This is where the network applications, such as web browsers or email programs, operate.
- Some of the most common application layer protocols are:
  - FTP (File Transfer Protocol): a standard network protocol that is used to transfer computer files from one host to another.
  - HTTP (Hypertext Transfer Protocol): HTTP is the underlying protocol used by the world wide web.
  - IMAP (Internet Message Access Protocol): IMAP is an internet standard protocol used by email clients to retrieve email messages from a mail server.
  - HTTPS (HTTP Secure): a protocol for secure communication over a computer network.
  - SMTP (Simple Mail Transfer Protocol): a TCP/IP protocol used in sending and receiving email. As it is limited in its ability to queue messages at the receiving end, it is usually used with one of two other protocols, POP3 or IMAP.
  - SNMP (Simple Network Management Protocol): created as a way of gathering information from different networked systems in a consistent way.

The transport layer

- Below the application layer is the transport layer. It is the main interface for all network applications.
- This layer sets up the communication between two hosts whereby they agree settings such as language and size of packets.
- The most commonly used transport layer protocols are:
  - TCP
  - UDP.
- The differences between TCP and UDP are:

TCP	UDP
Data is read as a byte stream. No distinguishing indications are transmitted to signal the message (segment) boundaries. TCP is a connection-oriented protocol. If a connection is lost, the server requests the lost part.	UDP is a connectionless protocol. When data or messages are sent, there is no guarantee they will arrive. There may also be corruption while transferring a message. Packets are sent individually and are guaranteed to be whole if they arrive. There is one packet per read call.
TCP is more complex but reliable.	UDP is faster but provides no reliability mechanism.
TCP is suited for applications that require high reliability, and where transmission time is relatively less critical.	UDP is suitable for applications that need fast, efficient transmission, such as games. UDP is also useful for servers that answer small queries from huge numbers of clients.
If two messages are sent along a connection, one after the other, the first message arrives first. Data cannot arrive in the wrong order.	Messages are not ordered. When two messages are sent out they may arrive in a different order. If ordering is required, it has to be managed by the application layer.
Data is read as a 'stream', with nothing distinguishing where one packet ends and the next begins. There may be multiple packets per read call.	There is no tracking of connections, etc. UDP is faster because there is no error checking for packets and the network card/OS has less work to do to translate the data back from the sent packets.

The network layer

- The network layer provides an interface with the physical network.
- The network layer is responsible for routing, which is moving packets across the network using the most appropriate paths.
- It also addresses messages and translates logical addresses (i.e. IP addresses) into physical addresses (i.e. MAC addresses). The main purpose of this layer is to organise or handle the movement of data on the network.
- The main protocol used at this layer is IP.
- This layer also formats the data for transmission and provides error control for data delivered on the physical network.

The data link layer

- The data link layer is sometimes known as the network interface layer.
- The data link layer is where most LAN and wireless LAN technologies are defined.
- This layer normally consists of device drivers in the OS and the network interface card attached to the system.
- The data link layer is the protocol layer in a program that handles the moving of data in and out across a physical link in a network.
- The device drivers and the network interface card control all communications with the media being used and transfer the data over the network.
- The most commonly used data link layer protocols are:
  - ARP (Address Resolution Protocol)
  - PPP (Point to Point Protocol).
- The data link layer is responsible for encoding bits into packets prior to transmission and then decoding the packets back into bits at the destination.
- The data link layer is also responsible for logical link control, media access control, hardware addressing, error detection and handling and defining physical layer standards.
- The data link layer processes data faster than the network layer because less analysis of the packet is required.

Data packets

- Anything sent between computers has to be divided up into what are called packets.
- Packets are small data units.
- Transmitted packets have to be put back together in the correct order.
- These protocols wrap each data packet with a set of instructions.
- The name for this is encapsulation.
- Once all the packets have been received, the client needs to know they have all arrived so the very last packet is a special one called a frame.

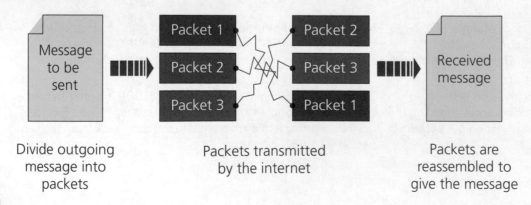

Divide outgoing message into packets

Packets transmitted by the internet

Packets are reassembled to give the message

Email protocols

- When you send and receive an email there are three different protocols that can be used to handle the email:
  - IMAP
  - POP
  - SMTP.
- IMAP and POP are used to receive mail; SMTP is used to send mail.

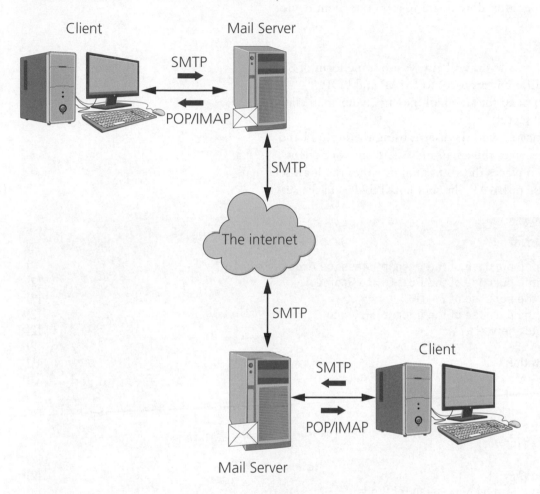

Receiving emails

- The software you use on your local machine is called a client, and this is connected to what is called a mail server.
- When someone sends you an email it travels from the sender's email client to their mail server using SMTP.
- Their mail server then uses the recipient's email address to determine where the mail should be sent and then delivers it to the receiver's mail server.
- The receiver's mail server stores the received email in a mailbox until the receiver's mail client asks for it.
- IMAP and POP are the two main protocols used for retrieving email from a mail server.
- Both protocols are supported by almost all popular mail client programs.
- The IMAP protocol, by default, allows the user to keep all messages on the server.
- It constantly synchronises the email client program with the server and displays what messages are currently there. All the actions performed on the messages are carried out directly on the server.

- The POP protocol is set by default to download all the messages from the email server onto the client device.
- This means that all the actions performed on the messages (reading, moving, deleting and so on) are performed on the client machine.
- Because everything is kept on the client machine, the user cannot reopen messages from any machine other than where the messages have been downloaded.
- There is an option to set up the POP protocol to save a copy of the message on the server after downloading it on the client device.

Sending emails

- When you send an email you will always use some form of SMTP, which is a totally different protocol to IMAP and POP.
- When you click on Send for an email message, your mail client contacts the SMTP server.
- The server authenticates who the user is using the login id and password, then it receives the email message from your client.
- The mail client then places the sent email in either the local sent mail folder or, in the case of IMAP, the sent email folder on the server.

Exam practice

1 Briefly describe the purpose of the Internet Message Access Protocol. [2]
2 Briefly describe the purpose of the Post Office Protocol. [2]
3 Briefly describe the purpose of SMTP. [2]
4 Briefly describe the purpose of the Internet Protocol. [2]
5 What is a computer network? [2]
6 What is a file server? [2]
7 What is a workstation? [1]
8 WAN stands for: [1]
   a) Wap Area Network
   b) Wide Area Network
   c) Wide Array Net
   d) Wireless Area Network.
9 What are routers? [2]
10 What are switches? [2]
11 State two different data transmission methods. [2]
12 What is a network topology? [2]
13 List five advantages and five disadvantages of using computer networks. [10]

Answers on pp. 121–2

ANSWERS CHECKED ☐

5.2 Network security

Specification references

You must be able to:

5.2.1 demonstrate an understanding of the importance of network security and be able to use appropriate validation and authentication techniques (access control, physical security and firewalls)

5.2.2 demonstrate an understanding of security issues associated with the cloud and other contemporary storage

5.2.3 demonstrate an understanding of different forms of cyber attack (based on technical weaknesses and behaviour) including social engineering (phishing, shoulder surfing), unpatched software, USB devices, digital devices and eavesdropping

5.2.4 demonstrate an understanding of methods of identifying vulnerabilities including penetration testing, ethical hacking, commercial analysis tools and review of network and user policies

5.2.5 demonstrate an understanding of how to protect software systems from cyber attacks, including considerations at the design stage, audit trails, securing operating systems, code reviews to remove code vulnerabilities in programming languages and bad programming practices, modular testing and effective network security provision

Testing

REVISED

- Penetration testing is the process of attempting to gain access to resources without knowledge of usernames, passwords and other normal means of access.
- The aim of a white-box penetration test is to simulate a malicious insider who has knowledge of and possibly basic credentials for the target system.
- The aim of a black-box penetration test is to simulate an external hack or cyber warfare attack.

Social engineering

REVISED

- Social engineering is a non-technical method used by hackers to gain access to data and to systems. It relies heavily on human interaction and often involves tricking people into breaking normal security procedures.
- Virus writers use social engineering to persuade people to run malware-laden email attachments.
- Phishers use social engineering to convince people to give them sensitive personal information.
- Scareware hackers use social engineering to frighten people into running software that is useless at best and dangerous at worst.

Blagging

- Blagging is the act of creating and using an invented scenario to engage a targeted victim in a manner that increases the chance the victim will divulge information or perform actions that would be unlikely in ordinary circumstances.

Phishing

- Phishing is used to attempt to persuade someone to enter confidential data, for example usernames, passwords and credit card details, by pretending to be from a trustworthy source.
- It is usually carried out by email spoofing or instant messaging. Users are often asked to enter details at a fake website which looks just like the proper version.

Pharming

- Pharming is a scamming practice in which malicious code is installed on a personal computer or server, or DNS records are modified, misdirecting users to fraudulent websites without their knowledge or consent.

Shouldering (or shoulder surfing)

- Shouldering, also sometimes called 'shoulder surfing', is using direct observation techniques, such as looking over someone's shoulder, to get passwords, PINs, security codes and similar personal data.

Malware

REVISED

- Malware is an umbrella term used to refer to a variety of forms of hostile or intrusive software. Malware includes computer viruses, worms, trojan horses, ransomware, spyware, adware, scareware and other malicious programs.
- Viruses, keyloggers, worms and many other software attacks are different types of malicious code.
- They are often confused and thought of as being the same thing.
- They are pieces of code that are able to replicate themselves.
- However, they are distinctly different with respect to the techniques they use and their host system requirements. This distinction is due to the way they attack the host systems.

Adware	Also known as advertising-supported software. This is any software package that automatically shows adverts, such as a pop-up. They may also be in the user interface of a software package or on an installation screen. The main object of adware is to generate revenue for its author. Adware, by itself, is harmless. However, some adware may include spyware such as keyloggers.
Computer virus	A computer virus is a self-replicating program that attaches itself to existing programs and can then easily spread from one computer to another.
	Viruses can increase their chances of spreading to other computers by linking to files on a network system. A virus attempts to make a computer system or data files unreliable.
Denial of service (DoS) attacks	This is an attempt to make a computer or network system unavailable to its users. A DoS attack is usually focused on preventing an internet site or service from functioning efficiently, or at all, temporarily or indefinitely. The attacks usually target sites or services hosted on high-profile web servers such as banks and payment websites (for example, PayPal).
Hacking	Hacking means finding out weaknesses in an established system and exploiting them. A computer hacker is a person who finds out weaknesses in a computer system to gain unauthorised access. A hacker may be motivated by a multitude of reasons, such as profit, protest or challenge.
Keyloggers	A keylogger is a type of spyware that logs the keys used and can collect data from an infected computer, including personal information such as websites visited, user logins and financial information.

- A trojan horse is non-replicating, malicious code contained inside what appears to be a useful program.
- A worm is a self-replicating program that does not alter files, but resides in active memory and propagates itself by means of computer networks to consume resources.
- Spyware is a non-replicating program used to track user activities, monitor their machines and relay personal information to attackers.
- A keylogger is a type of surveillance software that has the capability to record every keystroke the user makes.
- A file infector virus is malware that copies itself into other program files (.exe, .dll, .bin, .sys, .com, .drv). When the infected file is executed, it loads into memory and tries to infect other files. It is also known as a parasitic virus.
- A polymorphic virus is malware that changes its form each time it is executed, avoiding detection/removal by anti-virus software.
- A virus hoax is an email message that warns users of a non-existent virus or other malware.

Protection

Measures for protecting your personal data from cyber attacks

- Do not give out personal information over the phone, on the web or in an email unless completely sure of the recipient. Always verify the authenticity of requests for any personal information.
- Encrypt your data.
- Keep your operating system, browser, anti-virus and other critical software up to date.
- Never click on links in emails. Even if you do think the email is legitimate, go to the website and log on directly. Be suspicious of any unknown links or requests sent through email or text messages.
- Never open email attachments unless you know they are from a reliable source; turn off the option to automatically download attachments in emails.
- Set secure passwords and don't share them with anyone.
- Avoid using common words, phrases or personal information in your passwords.

Measures for protecting a network and computers from cyber attacks

- Encrypt the data.
- Ensure that any HTTP open sessions **time out** after a reasonable time.
- Ensure that TCP connections time out after a reasonable time.
- Install a firewall.
- Install anti-malware and anti-virus protection.
- Lock the network. Many cyber attack victims are compromised via Wi-Fi networks.
- The best defence against this is to have no wireless network at all. Wired networks, while less versatile due to the need for cables, are more secure. If you use Wi-Fi, update it regularly to the latest encryption standard.
- Secure the hardware. Physically locking computers to a desk using the small metal loop found on most laptop and desktop devices prevents theft and access to network login data.
- Use tracking software on all networked mobile devices.

> A **time-out** is where the server is set to think that there has been too long an interval of time between (1) the establishment of a connection, and (2) the receipt of any data, so the server drops the connection.

Common security attacks and countermeasures

- Common security attacks and countermeasures include:
  - firewalls
  - encryption
  - intrusion detection systems
  - unlicensed computer professionals
  - deep linking
  - cookies
  - denial of service attacks
  - TCP attacks
  - packet sniffing
  - social problems.

Firewalls

- The basic problem:
  - Many network applications and protocols have security problems that are fixed over time.
  - It is difficult for users to keep up with changes and keep hosts secure.
- Solution:
  - Administrators limit access to end hosts by using a firewall.
  - Firewalls are kept up to date by administrators.
- A firewall is a network security system that monitors and controls all incoming and outgoing network data transfers based on a set of what are called security rules.
- Firewalls can be either hardware or software:
  - Hardware firewalls can be purchased as standalone hardware but they are also often found in broadband routers.
  - Software firewalls are software based and must be installed on the computer. The software can then be customised.
- There are a number of techniques firewalls use to prevent harmful information from getting through the security wall. These include:
  - packet filtering: looking at the data in each packet entering or leaving the network
  - application gateway filtering: applying security mechanisms or blocking services such as FTP
  - proxy server filtering: intercepting all messages entering and leaving the network and hiding the true network address.
- In addition to limiting access to computers and the networks they are connected to, firewalls can be used to allow remote access to a private network using secure authentication.

Encryption

- Encryption is required when someone enters personal information or banking information on the internet to make a purchase.
- But the same encryption that can be of benefit can be of use to a terrorist.
- Even the information that you enter through an encrypted connection could be accessible online by a criminal.

Intrusion detection

- Used to monitor for suspicious activity on a network.
- Can protect against known software exploits, like buffer overflows.

Unlicensed computer professionals

- Plumbers and electricians, doctors and most other people who provide a service to the public are usually licensed by law. Computer professionals are not.
- This makes it almost impossible to know whether the person who is fixing your computer is competent and reliable.
- Remember that people accessing your computer have full access to all of the data on it.

Deep linking

- Users of the world wide web often move from page to page following hyperlinks, which can appear as images or text. Originally, hyperlinks were at the heart of the world wide web.
- Sometimes the hyperlink takes a user away from the website they are on to another website.
- Deep linking occurs when one web page includes a hyperlink to a web page that is buried deep within another site. This can give the appearance that the hyperlinked pages are part of the original website.
- A growing number of companies are concerned that their data will be stolen.

Cookies

- Internet cookies are very small text files.
- They are downloaded from the web server to a web browser.
- They record the activities on the browser, and then send them back to the server. Whilst cookies can be very useful for autocompleting forms, they can also be used by advertisers and less scrupulous users.

TCP attacks

- Recall how IP works: end hosts create IP packets and routers process them purely based on their destination address.
- The problem:
  - end hosts may lie about other fields which do not affect delivery
  - the host may use the source address to trick the destination into believing that the packet is from a trusted source, especially in applications which use IP addresses as a simple authentication method.
- The solution:
  - use better authentication methods.
- TCP connections have associated state information:
  - starting sequence numbers
  - port numbers.
- Port numbers are sometimes well known to begin with (for example, HTTP uses port 80).
- Sequence numbers are sometimes chosen in very predictable ways.
- If an attacker learns the associated TCP state for the connection, then the connection can be hijacked!
- The attacker can insert malicious data into the TCP stream, and the recipient will believe it came from the original source.
- For example, instead of downloading and running a new program, you download a virus and execute it.

Packet sniffing

- When someone wants to send a packet, they put the bits on the wire with the destination MAC address.
- Remember that other hosts are listening on the wire to detect for collisions.
- It couldn't get any easier to figure out what data is being transmitted over the network!

MAC address filtering

- Media access control (MAC) addresses identify every device on your network.
- A MAC address is an alphanumeric string separated by colons, like this: 00:03:D1:1A:2D:14.
- Networked devices use this address as identification when they send and receive data over the network.
- In MAC address filtering you find the MAC address of every device you want to allow on your network, and then you fill out a table in the router's user interface so that only devices on the list can join your network.

Social problems

- People can be just as dangerous as unprotected computer systems.
- People can be lied to, manipulated, bribed, threatened, harmed, tortured, etc. to give up valuable information.
- Most humans will break down once they are at the 'harmed' stage, unless they have been specially trained.

Automatic updates and patches

- If your device seems to be working fine, you may wonder why you should apply a patch or software update.
- By not applying a patch you might be leaving the door open for malware to come in.
- Malware exploits flaws in a system in order to do its work, and updates and patches are designed to close these doors as they are found.

Passwords

- Passwords are inconvenient, but necessary to protect your personal data.
- If you use the same password on all your devices and accounts, your data and your devices will also be vulnerable to malware and hackers.

Security misconfiguration vulnerabilities

- When any of the components that make up a web application are configured badly, there is a target for attackers.
- Security misconfiguration vulnerabilities can happen at platform level, web server level, application server level and through custom code.
- In order to provide a secure system, all of the component parts of a network application need to be configured correctly.
- There are many ways that misconfiguration can lead to security vulnerabilities.

- To protect from these vulnerabilities there are a number of steps that need to be taken:
  - ○ Keep software up to date by installing the latest updates and security patches.
  - ○ Remove unused features, including the removal of all the sample applications that come with content delivery systems.
  - ○ Disable default accounts and change passwords. You should also change usernames, passwords and ports for default accounts.
  - ○ Develop a strong application architecture that effectively isolates components and encrypts data. Ensure security settings are set to secure values.
  - ○ Run tools, such as automated scanners, to check for vulnerabilities.
  - ○ Secure all layers individually and don't rely on one layer in a web application providing security for layers lower down in the stack.

Unpatched and/or outdated software vulnerabilities

- Software vulnerabilities, like malware, have serious security implications.
- The companies that sell software are aware of these security vulnerabilities and regularly release security updates to address these flaws.
- Outdated and unpatched devices present a major security risk as the unpatched software remains weak, leaving the user open to cybercrime.
- Updating systems with the latest security patches protects against attacks that exploit vulnerabilities.
- Applying security updates often also addresses technical issues with the software and often improves the software's performance.

CAPTCHA

- CAPTCHA stands for Completely Automated Public Turing test to tell Computers and Humans Apart.
- It is a program used by some websites to provide further protection for a user's password by verifying that user input is not computer generated.
- There are now a wide number of different CAPTCHA systems using images, numbers and even simple calculations, but basically the idea is to create something humans can read but that current computer programs can't.

Email verification

- Email confirmation and CAPTCHA are used to solve different problems.
- Email verification is used to check that users are using their real email address in the registration process.
- Email verification is where an email is sent to the user's email address and they have to click on a link in it to confirm that the email address is theirs.
- Email confirmation also protects from identity theft.
- For example, the user cannot register a government email address.

Mobile phone verification

- With mobile phone verification, you ask the user to enter their mobile phone number.
- Then you send them an SMS (text message) with a code and they must enter this code into a web form on the website.

Exam practice

1 Briefly describe the two main functions of a computer virus.   [4]
2 Explain with examples the term 'computer virus'.   [6]
3 Describe the term 'trojan horse'.   [2]
4 State how worms differ from viruses.   [2]
5 State what the term 'spyware' refers to.   [2]
6 State what the term 'adware' refers to.   [2]
7 Describe the term 'insider attack'.   [2]
8 List four possible threats to a computer system and four possible security measures.   [4]
9 Briefly describe why a user should apply patches and updates to their software.   [6]
10 A school decides to block communication with websites that do not use HTTPS.
    Discuss the term 'HTTPS'.   [6]
11 Briefly describe the term 'phishing'.   [2]
12 Briefly describe the term 'shoulder surfing'.   [2]
13 Briefly describe the term 'pharming'.   [3]
14 Briefly describe the term 'spam'.   [2]
15 Describe the term 'spoofing'.   [3]
16 State what is meant by the term 'impersonation'.   [2]

Answers on pp. 122–3

ANSWERS CHECKED

5.3 The internet and the world wide web

Specification references

You must be able to:

5.3.1 demonstrate an understanding of what is meant by the internet and how the internet is structured (IP addressing, routers)

5.3.2 demonstrate an understanding of what is meant by the world wide web (WWW) and components of the WWW (web server, URLs, ISP, HTTP, HTTPS, HTML)

The world wide web

REVISED

- The world wide web (WWW) is made up of connected networks and computers where documents and other web resources are identified by URLs (uniform resource locators) and interlinked by hypertext links.
- It can be accessed via the internet.

HTTP

REVISED

- HTTP, the hypertext transfer protocol, is the foundation of data communication for the world wide web.
- Hypertext is structured text that uses logical links (hyperlinks) between nodes containing text.

HTTPS

REVISED

- Hypertext transfer protocol secure (HTTPS) is a secure version of HTTP.
- It means that all communications between your browser and the website will be encrypted.
- HTTPS uses one of two secure protocols to encrypt the data communications: SSL (secure sockets layer) or TLS (transport layer security).
- Both the TLS and SSL protocols use an asymmetric public key infrastructure (PKI) system.
- When your browser requests an HTTPS connection, the website will first send its SSL certificate to your browser. This certificate contains the public key needed to begin a secure data session.
- Based on this initial exchange, your browser and the website then initiate the SSL handshake.

TCP/IP

- TCP/IP is a protocol which allows computers on different networks to communicate.
- TCP/IP is a pair of protocols:
  - TCP: transmission control protocol
  - IP: internet protocol.

IP addressing

- Every computer station on the internet must have an IP address.
- This IP address must be unique but is not encoded in the network interface. It is set by software in the computer.

Exam practice

1 What software do you need to create a web page? [2]
2 What is the web? [3]
3 What is a URL? [1]

Answers on p.123

ANSWERS CHECKED

6.1 Emerging trends, issues and impact

Specification references

You must be able to:

6.1.1 demonstrate an understanding of the environmental impact of technology (health, energy use, resources) on society

6.1.2 demonstrate an understanding of the ethical impact of using technology (privacy, inclusion, professionalism) on society

6.1.3 demonstrate an understanding of the legal impact of using technology (intellectual property, patents, licensing, open source and proprietary software, cyber security) on society

Ethical use

REVISED

- If you access, view or collect confidential material and/or personal information, it is your responsibility to maintain confidentiality.
- Do not share this information with unauthorised individuals.
- **Ethics** relate to the rules and standards governing the conduct of an individual with others.
- As technology and computers became more and more a part of our everyday lives the definition of ethics evolved, called computer ethics.
- Computer ethics are concerned with standards of conduct as they relate to computers.
- But ethics and the law are not the same thing:

> Computer **ethics** are moral guidelines that govern the use of computers and information systems.

Ethics	The law
Ethics are a guideline to computer users and are not legally enforceable.	The law consists of rules to control computer users that are legally enforceable.
Computer users are free to follow or ignore a code of ethics.	Computer users must follow the regulations and law for the country they live in.
Ethical rules are universal and can be applied anywhere, all over the world.	Laws depend on the country and state where the crime is committed. There are many examples of laws in one country allowing things that are illegal in others. This is a big issue with the internet.
Ethics aims to create ethical computer users.	Laws aim to prevent misuse of computers.
If you don't follow ethical rules, you are deemed to be immoral.	Not obeying laws is referred to as crime.

The digital divide

- Over the past few years, society's dependence on computer technology has increased.
- The ability to communicate via email and access the internet has become an essential part of everyday life.
- But there are many people in the world who do not have access to the internet and this has led to a disparity called the digital divide. This gap is of growing concern.
- Rural communities, low income families, people with disabilities and large areas of the wider world do not have the same advantages as more privileged households and communities.
- To many people this is a major ethical issue.

> **Exam tip**
>
> Read through all the questions, quickly answering all the ones you definitely know first and leaving the hard ones until last.

Intellectual property

- There are laws relating to **copyright** and intellectual property.
- Intellectual property is about creations of the intellect (hence the name): inventions, artistic works, names, images and designs.
- Intellectual property also relates to industrial property, such as inventions, trademarks, etc.
- The word 'property' means a possession, something for which the owner has legal rights.
- Unlike intellectual property, copyright law only protects the form of expressions of ideas, not the ideas themselves. So copyright laws do not protect ideas or systems, only how they are expressed.
- This means that nothing in copyright laws prevents others from developing another work based on the same idea.

> **Copyright** is exclusive rights given to authors and artists to duplicate, publish and sell their materials.

Software theft

- Software theft occurs when someone:
  - steals software media
  - illegally copies a program
  - illegally registers and/or activates a program.

The environmental impacts of technology

- When you use computer electronics, you are participating in one phase of that product's life.
- Before the product makes it to you, raw materials (resources) are taken (extracted) from the environment.
- These are then processed and manufactured into a product.
- The product is packaged and transported, again using valuable resources.
- The next stage is the use of the product and the energy needed for this use.
- The final stage is how you dispose of the device when you change it.

> **Exam tip**
>
> Remember to leave yourself some time at the end to go back over your answers and add in little notes or pieces of information about the topic. You never know, this could help bump you up a grade!

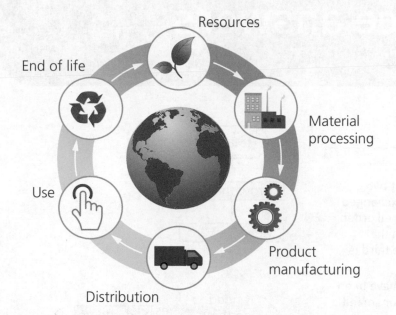

Resources

End of life

Material processing

Use

Product manufacturing

Distribution

What can individuals do?

- Everyone has a responsibility to reduce their individual carbon footprint.
- Completely powering off computing devices when not in use is good for your devices and for the planet.
- Other things that could be done include:
  - changing power settings so that devices power down after 15 minutes of inactivity
  - considering end-of-life management for all computing devices
  - dimming the screens on computing devices as this saves power
  - disabling screen savers as they don't actually conserve energy, some even use more energy than normal use
  - not having too many programs running at the same time, and changing the system settings to reduce programs that auto-start
  - shutting down all devices at the end of the working day
  - turning off printers, scanners and other peripherals when not using them
  - unplugging all computing devices when they are fully charged, otherwise they will be using power to keep topping themselves up throughout the day
  - unplugging chargers when they're not in use to save on power consumption
  - using hibernate instead of sleep mode.

Exam practice

1 Discuss the recent changes in shopping and shopping habits due to computing advancements. [6]
2 Discuss the issues around personal web security. [8]

Answers on pp. 123-4

ANSWERS CHECKED

Exam practice answers

1.1 Algorithms

1 (d) Traversal

2 A bubble sort is a sort in which the first two items to be sorted are examined and exchanged if necessary to place them in the required order. The second item is then compared with the third (exchanging them if required); the third is compared with the fourth.

The process is repeated until all pairs have been examined and all items are in the proper sorted order.

3 A merge sort cuts the array in half, sorting the left half and the right half independently, then merging together the two sorted halves.

4 (a) Sorting

5
```
RECEIVE length FROM (INT) KEYBOARD
RECEIVE breadth FROM (INT) KEYBOARD
area = length * breadth
SEND area TO DISPLAY
```

6 The basic building blocks are: sequential, selection and looping.
- Sequential: Set, input and output statements
- Selection: Conditional, if and if–else statements
- Looping: Iteration, while loops

7

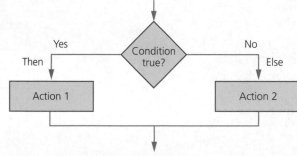

8

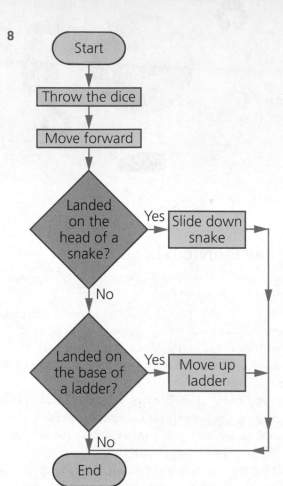

9 (c) High level

10 It is simple and useful when the elements to be searched are not in any definite order.

11 (d) The item is the last element in the array or is not there at all

12 (a) The item is somewhere in the middle of the array

13 Linear search; binary search

14 This search method starts at the beginning of the list and compares each element in turn with the required value until a match is found or the end of the list is reached.

15 (d) None of above

16 (c) Arrays

17 (b) Searching

1.2 Decomposition and abstraction

1 Syntax: `RECEIVE <identifier> FROM (type) <device>`

Examples:

```
RECEIVE Name FROM (STRING)
KEYBOARD
RECEIVE LengthOfJourney FROM
(INTEGER) CARD _ READER
RECEIVE YesNo FROM (CHARACTER)
CARD _ READER
```

2 Syntax: `SEND <expression> TO DISPLAY`

Example:

```
SEND 'Have a good day.' TO DISPLAY
```

3 Input is data that you enter into your computer. This can be entering text on the keyboard, moving the mouse or clicking the mouse button, or it can be as complex as scanning a document or downloading photos from a digital camera.

4 Output is anything that comes out of a computer. This can be numbers, characters, pictures, sound or printed pages.

2.1 Develop code

1 Syntax, runtime, logic

2 The correct name is 'syntax error' and it relates to the grammar rules of the programming language used. These errors are usually due to using the wrong case, placing punctuation in positions where it should not exist or failing to insert punctuation where it should be placed within the code.

3 Called 'runtime errors', these occur whenever the program instructs the computer to carry out an operation that it is either not designed to do or slow to do. This causes a crash or slow running of the code.

4 Logic errors are the most difficult kind of errors to detect and rectify. This is usually down to the fact that there is no obvious indication of the error within the software. The program will run successfully; however, it will not behave in the manner it was designed to. In other words, it will simply produce incorrect results.

5 Dry-run testing is usually carried out on the algorithm, which is written in pseudo-code or as part of a flowchart. This form of testing is usually done prior to the program code being written.

6 A trace table is a technique used to test algorithms to see if any logic errors are occurring whilst the algorithm is being processed. Within the table, each column contains a variable and each row displays each numerical input into the algorithm and the resultant values of the variables.

7 (b) Debugging

8 It is a measure of the amount of time for an algorithm to execute.

9 It must work, and it must complete its task in a finite (reasonable) amount of time.

10 (c) Time and space

11 (b) Counting the number of key operations

2.2 Constructs

1
```
SET n TO 1
WHILE n <= 50
    SEND n TO DISPLAY
    DO SET n TO n + 1
END WHILE
```

2
```
FOR n = 1 TO 60 STEP 1
    SEND n TO DISPLAY
END FOR
```

3 It is an independent set of statements which can be called in another program. Each program segment is called a module.

4
```
SEND 'Please enter two numbers' TO
DISPLAY
RECEIVE start FROM (INT) KEYBOARD
RECEIVE finish FROM (INT) KEYBOARD
FOR n = start TO finish STEP 1
    SEND n TO DISPLAY
END FOR
```

5
```
SEND 'Please enter the start number'
TO DISPLAY
RECEIVE start FROM (INT) KEYBOARD
SEND 'Please enter the end number' TO
DISPLAY
RECEIVE finish FROM (INT) KEYBOARD
IF start > finish THEN
    SEND 'Your start number is larger
    than your end number' TO DISPLAY
ELSE
    FOR n = start TO finish STEP 1
        SEND n TO DISPLAY
    END FOR
END IF
```

6
```
SET a TO 1
REPEAT
    SEND a TO DISPLAY
    SET a TO a + 1
UNTIL a = 6    #will output 1, 2, 3,
               #4, 5, 6
```

7
```
SET a TO 1
WHILE a < 4
    SEND a TO DISPLAY
```

```
    DO SET a TO a + 1
END WHILE    #will output 1, 2, 3
```
8
```
FOR a = 1 TO 3 STEP 1
    SEND a TO DISPLAY
END FOR    # will output 1, 2, 3
```

2.3 Data types and structures

1 A string or text data type is capable of holding any alphanumeric character whether it is text, numbers or symbols. It is also capable of storing non-printable characters such as carriage returns as well as punctuation characters and spaces.

2 Gives the length of the string; in this case it evaluates to 7.

3 Variables declared inside a block or function are said to belong only to that block and are called local variables. Values of these variables are valid only in that block.

4 Variables declared before the main function block are called global variables. Values of these variables are available in every block of the program.

5 Evaluates to 'programmingiscool'.

6 Changes an integer to a string. In this case evaluates to the string '16'.

7 −9, 3, 5, 8, 98, 5, 103.

8 Processing speed: The time it takes a computer to calculate using real numbers is a lot longer than using whole numbers as held in integer data types.

Storage: Real data types take up more memory than integer data types; therefore, if decimal points are not required it is better to use integers.

9 A real data type contains numeric data in a decimal form. It is used in situations where more accurate information is required than an integer can provide, as an integer is a whole number.

10 Converts a string to a real number. In this case evaluates to the number 1.3.

11 Changes a string to an integer. In this case it evaluates to the integer 16.

12 `primes = [2, 3, 5, 7, 11, 13]`

13 (a) relatively permanent collections of data

14 `primes[5] = 17   # array is now [2, 3,`
`                  # 5, 7, 11, 17]`

15 A one-dimensional array is a list of variables. To create an array, you first must define an array variable of the desired type. One-dimensional arrays in Python and PHP are a data structure that allows a list of items to be stored with the capability of accessing each item by pointing to its location within the array, for example:
```
carMakers = ['Ford', 'Land Rover',
'Vauxhall', 'Nissan', 'Toyota']
```

16 Two-dimensional arrays are a little more complex than the one-dimensional versions above, but really they are nothing more than an array of arrays; in other words, an array in one row and another in the next row.

17 It is common practice within programming for the first element within an array to be given an index of 0 rather than 1, because 0 is considered by most mathematicians to be an integer between −1 and 1 and so in languages where arrays are positively indexed, 0 is the first number (−1 is not possible, so the first possible value is 0).

18 In this way the computer only needs to keep track of the address of the first element; the addresses of other elements can be calculated.

19
```
tables = [[1, 2, 3],
          [2, 4, 6],
          [3, 6, 9],
          [4, 8, 12]]
```

20 9

2.4 Input/output

1 Sequential text files are stored like a one-dimensional array but they are read from start to finish and so cannot be read from and written to simultaneously. They are readable across systems because they have a universal standard format that is used in all text editors.

Numerical data is always stored as a string; for example, 5.32 would be stored as '5.32'.

2 Accessing data sequentially is much faster than accessing it randomly because of the way in which the disk hardware works. Because reading randomly involves a higher number of seek operations than a sequential read, random reads deliver a lower rate of throughput. The same is true for random writing.

2.5 Operators

1
```
RECEIVE length FROM (INT) KEYBOARD
RECEIVE breadth FROM (INT) KEYBOARD
area = length * breadth
perimeter = 2*(length + breadth)
SEND area TO DISPLAY
SEND perimeter TO DISPLAY
```

2
```
SEND 'Please enter a number' TO
DISPLAY
RECEIVE number FROM (INT) KEYBOARD
IF (number MOD 2) = 0 THEN
    SEND 'even' TO DISPLAY
ELSE
    SEND 'odd' TO DISPLAY
END IF
```

3

Operator	Description
>	greater than
<	less than
=	equal to
>=	greater than or equal to
<=	less than or equal to
!=	not equal to

4
```
SEND 'Please enter the size of your
square' TO DISPLAY
RECEIVE side FROM (INT) KEYBOARD
IF side < 0
    SEND 'Length entered must be
    positive' TO DISPLAY
ELSE
    SEND side*side TO DISPLAY
END IF
```

5
```
SEND 'Please enter three numbers, one
at a time' TO DISPLAY
RECEIVE a FROM (INT) KEYBOARD
RECEIVE b FROM (INT) KEYBOARD
RECEIVE c FROM (INT) KEYBOARD
IF (a = b) and (a = c)
    SEND 'all 3 equal' TO DISPLAY
ELSE
    SEND 'not all equal' TO DISPLAY
END IF
```

6
```
SEND 'Please enter three numbers, one
at a time' TO DISPLAY
RECEIVE a FROM (INT) KEYBOARD
RECEIVE b FROM (INT) KEYBOARD
RECEIVE c FROM (INT) KEYBOARD
IF a > b
    bigab = a
ELSE
    bigab = b
END IF
IF c > bigab
    SEND c TO DISPLAY
ELSE
    SEND bigab TO DISPLAY
END IF
```

7 (b) logical operation

8

Operator	Description
MOD	modulo
–	subtraction
×	multiplication
DIV	integer division

9 `9 DIV 5  # evaluates to 1`

10 `9 MOD 5  # evaluates to 4`

2.6 Subprograms

1 A function is a small segment of a program (a subprogram) designed to perform a specific task and return a result to the main or calling program.

2 A user-defined function is a complete and independent program unit which can be used (or invoked) by the main program or by other subprograms. If there are a number of statements that are repeatedly needed in the same program at different locations then a function may be used.

3 Once a function is created it can be called from the main program or from any other function. This main program or the function which calls another function is called the calling function.

4 Information or values are passed to a function through special identifiers called arguments.

5 The arguments (values) which are passed to the function when a function call is made are called actual parameters.

6 The arguments which are used in the argument list of the function header to receive the values from the calling program are called formal parameters or dummy parameters.

7 A function is invoked (or called) through an output statement or through an assignment statement by using the function name followed by the list of arguments. For example, `p = prod(x, y)`.

8 Sequence, selection, iteration.

9 It is a method of using the concepts of sequence, selection, iteration and modularity.

10 Modifications are limited to a particular module; increases programmer productivity.

11 Structured programs are easy to write as the programming logic is well organised. Structured programs are easy to test and debug.

12 To produce error-free programs; to incorporate basic structured constructs; to obtain a disciplined approach towards programming; to improve the flexibility of a program.

13 A structure is a group of data of different data types.

14 An array of structures contains data elements of structure type stored in an array.

15
```
n = 1
WHILE n ≤ 50
    SEND n TO DISPLAY
    n = n + 1
END WHILE
```

16
```
FOR n = 1 TO 60
    SEND n TO DISPLAY
END FOR
```

17
```
SEND 'Please enter two numbers' TO
DISPLAY
RECEIVE start FROM (INT) KEYBOARD
RECEIVE finish FROM (INT) KEYBOARD
FOR n = start to finish
    SEND n TO DISPLAY
END FOR
```

18
```
SEND 'Please enter the start number'
TO DISPLAY
RECEIVE start FROM (INT) KEYBOARD
SEND 'Please enter the end number'
TO DISPLAY
RECEIVE finish FROM (INT) KEYBOARD
IF start > finish
    SEND 'Your start number is larger
    than your end number' TO DISPLAY
ELSE
    FOR n = start to finish
        SEND n TO DISPLAY
    END FOR
END IF
```

3.1 Binary

1

Addition	Answer
101 + 11 =	00001000
111 + 111 =	00001110
1010 + 1010 =	00010100
11101 + 1010 =	00100111
11111 + 11111 =	00111110

2 (a) binary

3 (c) decimal

4 (b) octal

5 (d) hexadecimal

6 (b) 1

3.2 Data representation

1 60 minutes/hour, 20 × 60 = 1200 minutes. So that's exactly 1200 MB, which is 1.2 GB.

2 In analogue recordings, the machine is constantly recording any sound or noise that is coming through the microphones. In digital recordings you don't have a constant recording, you have a series of samples or snapshots which are a measure of amplitude at a given point in time and are taken from the sound being recorded.

3 (a) American Standard Code for Information Interchange

4 (c) 7

5 Converts the character to a character code. In this case it evaluates to 97 using ASCII/Unicode.

6 Converts the character code to a character. In this case it evaluates to 'a' using ASCII/Unicode.

7 (a) ASCII

8 Extended ASCII uses all 8 bits whereas ASCII just uses 7. This means it can store more characters.

9 Unlike ASCII's 128 characters and 7 bits, Unicode can store each character with 32 bits so contains over 110,000 characters and has space for 1,114,111 different values. Because of this it can store foreign language characters. The first 128 characters are the same as ASCII.

10 Analogue data is continuous, analogous to the actual information it represents. For example, a mercury thermometer is an analogue device. The mercury rises in direct proportion to the temperature. Computers cannot work with analogue information.

Digital data breaks the information up into separate steps. This is done by breaking the analogue information into pieces and representing those pieces using binary digits.

11 (d) all of the above

12 Step 1, (length × breadth) × bit depth: (800 × 900) × 24 bits = 17280000 bits

Step 2, convert into appropriate units: 17280000/8 = 2160000 bytes; 2160000 bytes/1000 = 2160 kB; 2160 kB/1000 = 2.1 MB

13 800 × 600 is 480000 pixels. Each pixel takes 3 bytes (one byte each for red/green/blue), so 480000 × 3 is 1440000 bytes overall, which is approximately 1.4 MB, therefore this is the space required for the image in RAM.

On disk, a JPEG file takes up much less space than that due to compression, which is an effective space-saving technique for image and audio data.

3.3 Data storage and compression

1 (c) 4 bits

2 It refers to the number of bits processed by a computer's CPU in one go. It used to be 8 bits, but with modern CPUs it is now typically 32 or 64 bits.

3 (d) 1 KB = 1000 bytes

4 (a) Binary digit

5 (c) 8 bits

6 (a) 1000 bytes

7 (c) 1000 megabytes

8 (b) petabyte

9 If we will look at a sentence such as 'Run-length encoding makes files smaller; smaller files use run-length encoding.' we would notice that each character and space in this sentence made up one unit of memory. So we would have a file size of 78 bytes. There are regular patterns in our sentence as most of the words appear twice with the exception of 'makes' and 'use' which appear just once. If we create a dictionary, we can catalogue the words so we do not need to repeat them, just call up the catalogue location.

10 Run-length encoding is a data compression algorithm used in most bitmap file formats. This system is used in TIFF, BMP and PCX file formats. RLE works by reducing the size of a repeating string. A repeating string is called a run and is typically encoded into two bytes. The first byte represents the number of characters in the run and is called the run count. The second byte is the value of the character in the run and is called the run value.

RLE is suitable for compressing any type of data. The problem is that the content of the data affects the compression ratio as it depends on the number of repeats in the string, the more repeats the more effective the compression.

11 Data compression is a set of steps for packing data into a smaller 'electronic space' (data bits). Compression results in much smaller storage space requirements and is often much faster for communications as compressed data works more effectively on our mobile phones and portable devices. But to be effective we still need to allow for the original data to be accessed and used. This is often achieved by eliminating the repetition of identical sets of data bits. We call this removing the 'redundancy'.

12 Sort symbols in descending order by frequency.

Merge the two least-frequent symbols, with lower symbol as root and combined frequency as frequency.

Repeat until tree is complete.

3.4 Encryption

1 7 6 7 0 5 7 14

2 Cryptographic algorithms are sequences of rules that are used to encrypt and decrypt code. They are algorithms that protect data by making sure that unwanted people can't access it.

3.5 Databases

1 Databases use a series of tables to store data. A table simply refers to a two-dimensional representation of data stored in rows and columns.

2 a) A table in a relational database is also referred to as a 'relation'. A relational database consists of two or more related tables.

b) In databases, records are a complete single set of information. Records are comprised of fields.

c) A row within a 'relation' table is an instance of one record.

d) Columns within a database table contain all the information of a single type, such as all the employees' names.

e) Within relational database tables, a field is a single snippet of data that is at the intersection of a row and a column.

f) A database query is fundamentally a question that you put to the database. The outcome of the query is the information that is returned by the database in answer to the question.

g) Every relational database should contain one or more columns that are assigned as the primary key.

3 Database indexes assist database management systems to find and sort records more quickly.

Indexes in databases can be compared to indexes in books. If you look at a book's index, it enables you to find the information you want quickly without having to read through the entire book. Within a database, the index enables the database software to search for and find data in a table without having to scan the whole table.

Indexes can be based on a single field or on multiple fields. Indexes that utilise a number of fields enable the user to distinguish between records in which the first field may have the same value.

Primary keys within tables are automatically indexed.

4.1 Machines and computational modelling

1 An input device is a peripheral (piece of computer hardware equipment) used to provide data and control signals to an information processing system such as a computer or other information appliance.

2 Output devices are hardware devices that allow information to be output from a computer, for example the monitor and speakers.

4.2 Hardware

1 (d) Arithmetic logic and control unit

2 Cache memory is a small and fast memory between the CPU and main memory. It is extremely fast compared to normal memory. Transferring data between main memory and the CPU causes delay because RAM is slower than CPU. Cache memory stores copies of data from the most frequently used main memory locations. When the processor needs to read from or write to a location in main memory, it first checks whether a copy of the data is in the cache. If so, the processor immediately reads or writes to cache. Computers use multiple levels of cache such as Level 1 and Level 2 cache. CPU-resident cache is known as L1 or primary cache (16 to 32 KB). Cache is also added to the motherboard, known as L2 cache (512 KB to 1024 KB). Higher-end systems can have as much as 2 MB of L2 cache on the motherboard.

3 (a) Input unit

4 (a) Electrically Erasable Programmable Read Only Memory

5 (a) ALU

6 (a) seek time + latency time

7 – CPU speed/clock speed: The clock speed is the number of instructions executed by the CPU in one second. It is measured in megahertz (million cycles per second). The average speed of a new CPU is about 1000 MHz to 4000 MHz. (1 to 4 gigahertz).

   – Instruction set: The number of instructions decides the efficiency of a CPU. The more instructions, the less efficient the CPU; fewer instructions mean a more efficient CPU.

   – Word size/register size: The size of registers determines the amount of data the computer can work with at a time. The smaller the size of the register, the slower the computer. It is also known as word size. It varies from 16 bits to 128 bits.

   – Data bus capacity: The width of a data bus determines the largest number of bits that can be transported at one time.

   – Cache memory size: Cache memory is a high-speed memory. The greater the cache, the faster a processor runs. Most modern processors can execute multiple instructions per clock cycle, which speeds up a program. Some CPUs have storage for instructions and data built inside the processor chip. This is called internal cache or L1 cache memory.

   – Memory size: The amount of primary storage (RAM) determines the size of program that can be kept in primary storage, which is faster than secondary storage, and thereby the speed of the computer increases. The size of RAM varies.

8 – Program counter: This register stores the address of the next instruction to be executed.

   – Memory address register (MAR): This register specifies the address in memory where information can be found. This register is also used to point to a memory location where information can be stored.

   – Memory buffer register: This register acts as an interface between CPU and memory. When the CPU issues a Read Memory command, the instruction is fetched and placed in the MB register.

9 (c) ALU

10 (d) all of these

11 (d) all of these

12 (d) Compact Disk Read Only Memory

13 (c) load a program from the disk into the memory

14 (d) all of these

15 They are used to store intermediate data and instructions.

16 It keeps track of the memory address of the instruction that is to be executed next.

17 (c) read-only memory chip

18 (d) any of the above

19 (d) microprocessor

20 (b) CD-ROM

21 (c) control unit, arithmetic logic unit and primary storage

22 (b) output unit

23 (a) Arithmetic Logic Unit

24 It carries a word to or from memory.

25 It carries a memory address. The width of the address bus equals the number of bits in the MAR.

26 (d) all of these

4.3 Logic

1 IF 'door is open' AND 'cold outside' THEN 'wear coat' or

IF door = 1 AND cold = 1 THEN coat

2
```
a = 2
REPEAT
    SEND a TO DISPLAY
    a = a + 2
UNTIL a = 102
```

3 The Boolean data type represents the values of true/false or yes/no. The primitive data type of a Boolean is logical. Boolean logic is a type of mathematical comparison. It is used to evaluate true or false.

4

The tyre is flat.	The wheel has been removed.	Take the wheel to the garage.
1	1	1
1	0	0
0	1	0
0	0	0

5

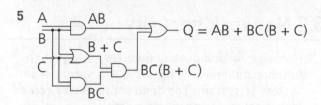

$$Q = AB + BC(B + C)$$

6 AND gate:

A	B	Q
0	0	0
0	1	0
1	0	0
1	1	1

OR gate:

A	B	Q
0	0	0
0	1	1
1	0	1
1	1	1

4.4 Software

1 The operating system is a collection of programs that control the system. It is responsible for the management and control of all the computer's resources. This includes memory, processors, hard drives, monitoring I/O devices, etc. It not only handles the system resources, it also handles the application software that users run, security and file management. It also provides a link between the hardware and software.

2 The operating system memory management functions include controlling the location of memory, and dealing with the transfer of programs in and out of memory when the process no longer needs it or when the process has been ended. It also carries out a process called scheduling where it manages the CPU, organising the use of memory between programs and processing time between programs and users. The OS also keeps track of processors and the status of any process running.

3 Peripheral management is one of the main functions of the operating system – managing the input to the CPU and the output from the CPU.

4 (d) entertainment software

5 (b) application software

6 (a) system software

7 (c) compiler

8 (c) diagnostic software

9 (d) assembly languages

10 (a) high-level language

4.5 Programming languages

1 (b) Object code is saved for future use.

2 (c) assembler

3 (c) compiler

4 (b) A compiler converts the whole of a higher-level program code into machine code in one step.

5 (a) machine language

5.1 Networks

1 IMAP is a mail retrieval protocol with improvements over POP. Its main advantage is that you can keep emails on the mail server instead of always downloading them.

2 POP is used for downloading emails to a local PC; it operates at the application layer.

3 Simple Mail Transfer Protocol is used for sending email; it operates at the application layer.

4 The Internet Protocol operates at the network layer of the OSI model and is involved in network routing and addressing.

5 A computer network can be defined as the interconnection of autonomous computers and terminals using communication systems to facilitate exchange of information.

6 A file server is the main component of a network. It is a very fast computer with a large amount of RAM and storage space. The file server stores all the files and application software and operating system.

7 Work stations (also referred to as clients) are the computers connected to the file server.

8 (b) Wide Area Network

9 A router translates information from one network to another. Routers select the best path to route a message based on the destination address and origin.

10 A switch is a device that provides a central connection point to cables from servers, workstations and peripherals.

11 Serial transmission and parallel transmission.

12 Network topology is the physical layout of the cables, arrangement of resources and communication facilities.

13 Advantages of using computer networks include:
- The network allows users to share software stored in a main system.
- Site (network) software licences are less expensive than buying several standalone licences.
- Files can easily be shared between users over a network.
- Network users can communicate via email, instant messenger and VoIP.
- Security over networks is of a high standard; i.e. users cannot see other users' files, unlike on standalone machines.
- Within networks, it is much more straightforward to backup data as it is all stored on the file server.
- Networks allow data to be transmitted to remote areas that are connected within local areas.
- Networking computers allows users to share common peripheral resources such as printers and fax machines, thereby saving money.

- The cost of computing is reduced per user as compared to the development and maintenance of a group of unnetworked standalone computers.

Disadvantages of using computer networks include:
- The cost of purchasing cabling to construct a network as well as the file servers can be expensive.
- The management of a large network is complicated, requiring training, and a specialist network manager usually needs to be employed.
- In the event of a file server breaking down, the files contained on the server become inaccessible, although email might still work if it is stored on a separate email server. The computers can still be used but are isolated.
- If a virus gets into the system through a network, it can easily spread to other computers.
- With networks, there is a risk of hacking, particularly with wide area networks. Stringent security measures are required to prevent such abuse such as a firewall.

5.2 Network security

1 Propagation and destruction. The propagation function defines how the virus will spread from system to system. The destructive power comes from implementing whatever malicious activity the virus writer had in mind.

2 Viruses are a collection of coded instructions which are self-replicating. When a virus attaches itself to another file it infects it. They are normally inactive until an infected program is run.

They are broadly classified into three categories:
- Boot infectors
- System infectors
- Executable program infectors.

Boot infectors create bad sectors. They remain in memory until the system is shutdown. System infectors infect the hard disk or bootable floppies, which may contain system files. Executable program infectors are dangerous and devastating. They spread to almost any executable program, attaching themselves to programming files.

3 A trojan horse is a malware program that appears benevolent but carries a malicious, behind-the-scenes payload that has the potential to wreak havoc on a system or network.

4 Worms replicate themselves without requiring any human intervention.

5 Spyware monitors your actions and transmits important details to a remote system that spies on your activity.

6 Adware uses a variety of techniques to display advertisements in the infected computer's active content.

7 An insider attack is a security breach that is caused or facilitated by someone who is a part of the very organisation that controls or builds the asset that should be protected.

8 Threats:
   – privacy
   – integrity
   – environmental damage
   – human threats
   – software threats
   – unauthorised access
   – computer viruses.
   Security:
   – physical protection of machine and media
   – using passwords and users
   – using licensed software
   – use of cryptography.

9 If your device seems to be working fine, you may wonder why you should apply a patch or software update. By not applying a patch you might be leaving the door open for malware to come in. Malware exploits flaws in a system in order to do its work, and updates and patches are designed to close these doors as they are found.

10 Both the TLS and SSL protocols use an asymmetric public key infrastructure (PKI) system. When the school's browser requests an HTTPS connection, the website will first send its SSL certificate to your browser. This certificate contains the public key needed to begin a secure data session. Based on this initial exchange, your browser and the website then initiate the SSL handshake.

11 Phishing is trying to trick someone into revealing confidential information, such as passwords and account numbers, by imitating a company or website the user would normally be familiar with.

12 Shoulder surfing is having someone steal confidential information simply by looking over your shoulder while you're accessing it.

13 Pharming is when a user is misdirected to an attack website, without their knowledge, by code that has been previously installed on their computer that modifies their destination URL to one chosen by the attacker.

14 Spam is unsolicited email. It is usually more of an annoyance than a security threat. Spam wastes time, employee resources and bandwidth.

15 Spoofing is a human or software-based attack in which the goal is to pretend to be someone else for the purpose of concealing their identity. Spoofing can occur by using IP addresses, a network adapter's hardware media access control (MAC) address and email.

16 Impersonation is a human-based attack in which an attacker pretends to be someone they are not.

5.3 The internet and the world wide web

1 You can make a web page in a text editor using basic HTML (HyperText Markup Language), as this is the code web pages are written in.

2 A global network of computers connected by wires (phone lines, cable lines, DSL, etc.). When people talk about the web, that is not the internet, just a piece of it. Email, chat rooms, newsgroups, FTP (File Transfer Protocol): all of these things make up the internet.

3 A URL or uniform resource locator is a reference or address for a certain company, server or file on the world wide web.

6.1 Emerging trends, issues and impact

1 In the last ten years there have been major changes in the way we shop due to new online shopping environments being launched, coupled with the expanding availability of super-fast broadband to people's homes. This now means that people can sit at home and buy the things that they want. The ease with which people can now shop has caused a big shift in the products that shoppers most desire. Recent statistics have shown that technology such as tablet computers and home communication packages (TV/broadband/phone) are the items most wanted by people living in the UK.

2 Some of the world's best security researchers have been threatened with legal action for their efforts to expose vulnerabilities in internet infrastructure. The law tries to prevent hacking, or breaking into private networks and systems. But internet security experts use hacking projects to uncover security flaws with the intention of fixing them. Many people believe that cybercrime

laws should take into account the intent behind hacking, and not just the act itself. We also willingly give up our personal data on a daily basis, to services such as Facebook and Google. In these cases, our data isn't being stolen from us. A key feature of the internet that affects our privacy is the net's inability to forget anything once posted there. Web pages about individuals often stay online and searchable indefinitely, potentially affecting the subject's reputation. Another way that every internet user's privacy is infringed is by government surveillance. The governments of most nations tap internet traffic as part of national security programmes. As with all moral issues about internet privacy, there are two sides to the story – that of the person giving up their private data, and that of the person storing it.